Reinardy

Seven Sacraments
in The Christian Community

D1807531

Seven Sacraments
in The Christian Community

Evelyn Francis Capel

Revised and edited by Tom Ravetz

Floris Books

First published by The Christian Community Press in 1949.
This extensively revised edition first published in 1999.

© The Christian Community, 1999

All rights reserved. No part of this publication may
be reproduced without the prior permission of
Floris Books, 15 Harrison Gardens, Edinburgh.

British Library CIP Data available

ISBN 0-86315-289-9

Printed in Great Britain
by WBC Book Manufacturers, Bridgend, Mid Glam.

Contents

Prologue

Asking questions is the beginning of wisdom, but the question 'why' is not always the best one to ask. There are more things in heaven and earth than ever went into the answer to the question 'why?' There are other questions that lead much further but they do not lie so ready to hand; they need to be found. They show themselves to those who look at the world and at life with seeing eyes. It is important to realize this when approaching the subject of the Christian sacraments from a modern point of view. It is easy enough to ask why we should have sacraments. But answers to such a question will all seem merely theoretical until they have seen, even if only in a glimpse, the place where sacraments belong in life and in the world. This place can be described from a number of angles and viewpoints but just as it is humanly possible only to walk along one path at a time if one needs to reach a set point, so it is with one's thoughts. The following line of thought is put forward as one of many paths leading towards a view of the world in which sacraments have their place.

The power to change

To be able to change is the greatest gift of human nature. It is both comforting and true to say of a child: they will grow out of it, or of a young person: it is only a stage, it will pass. It is equally true to say of adults that they will learn by experience as they grow older, they will be different. At the end of a lifetime many people can still say, 'If I had my time over again, how differently I would use it!' The nearness of death does not, in fact, bring to people the mood that all is finished and over. It brings the feeling that, even if it be awesome, now the greatest change of all is coming. The vital importance of the human power to change is the theme of one of the greatest plays about human life — Goethe's *Faust*. The hero is a learned man who, in despair about his life's lack of meaning, makes a pact with the Devil for his soul. The Devil is to give him the use of all his powers and magic in return for his soul at death. However, there is a condition attached on which the whole action of the play turns. The Devil has to succeed in making Faust so contented on earth that he will want to say to one moment in his life: stay, you are too beautiful to let go! In the event, despite the Devil's best efforts, Faust never comes to the point of saying these words because, whatever he experiences or achieves, there is still something beyond the present moment towards which he is urged. At the end of the drama the angels are able to rescue Faust's soul, just because he has never lost the will to go on and to change.

Throughout the whole of this play's two long parts, one describing Faust's descent into his lower self, the other his ascent towards the world of the angels, this is the main point. Why is Faust's refusal to be satisfied so significant?

Anyone who looks around in the world will make observations of the following kind. We are going to plant seeds in the garden. We bring them in little packets with labels which tell us what kind of plants will grow from them. If we are very observant we notice the shapes and colour of the seeds and learn for the future what a cabbage or sunflower seed is like. The next season we may even know, without the help of the packet, what to expect. However, we could never know this without having learnt it.

The ordinary human imagination is too limited to predict from the appearance of a seed what plant it will produce. Yet there is no power on earth which can persuade a cabbage seed to produce anything but a cabbage. It is predestined to this from the start. If we muddle up the seeds we will be surprised by what comes up, but the plants will only be developing along their own fixed lines. Plants go through wonderful, unimaginable changes as they grow, but they are changes to a fixed pattern. The plant does not change its own nature.

Another observation can be made with animals. When a ewe bears a lamb it is first of all a woolly creature, nestling up to its mother. As it grows stronger it skips in the field with the other lambs. No sooner is it full-grown than it settles down to be a proper old sheep, indistinguishable from those with years behind them. Animals have a short youth during which they change quickly, but these changes are only the process by which they reach their own type. When growth is over they exist in a continuous old age, following the habits of their kind. Like the plants they are predestined creatures. In some animals certain changes other than those they make of themselves are possible, it is true. They can be forced on them by change of environment or by training. But when all is said and done, these changes are not great and their limits are soon reached. It still holds good to say that each animal is predestined from birth to become what it becomes. Plants, animals and all the creatures of the earth that are not human are fixed in their nature and cannot change except to their own pattern. The power to change and to go on changing is the distinctive quality of the human being; it is this power which decides the destiny of Faust.

If, instead of observing the growth of a plant or an animal, one observes a growing child, the difference is at once apparent. A child is born very far from what it has to become, it is long helpless and in need of care. It is much less finished than an animal, but it has more to develop. At least twenty-one years are necessary for its growing-up. Children are born in reality not once but twice. They have to be born in body and in soul.

The first birth happens when the child's body leaves the mother's and begins its own life. The birth of the soul comes later. Little children live in their thoughts and feelings very much from what they receive. They are carried in a 'soul womb,' woven by parents and teachers, human nature as it is common to us all. Their own individuality is still far off from them in the distance until they grow out of childhood into youth.

Then, around the age of fourteen, the second birth occurs. The soul of the boy or girl begins its own independent life. Slowly all the thoughts, feelings and impulses to action which are present in a healthy grown-up soul are born. The individuality becomes more distinct. It may often be hidden, as it may still be hidden in many quite grown-up people, but it is hidden now within the soul whereas before it was outside. A twenty-one year old young man or woman who has gone through this long process of the twofold birth is grown-up and has changed considerably since the day when he or she was born. It has been a long process of changing, but does the change stop here? What do we think of someone who has not changed since the age of twenty-one? We feel that something is wrong, that it is a case of arrested development. When body and soul are fully born, then the changes that are brought about by the human spirit can properly begin.

There is a time of life when, in the course of nature, the third birth should be happening. Between twenty-one and twenty-eight the true self, or individuality, should emerge from the womb of the soul. However, the course of nature has less to do with this birth than with the other two. This is the moment when human souls have to will of themselves to change. Here the Devil begins to wait and watch for the moment when his Faust is tempted to say: I have had enough, let me go on just as I am.

When human beings have grown up, they have to become willing to die — that is, to let go what they have already become, to embrace the new and be born again. With the right experience we can know what plant will grow out of a certain seed, what mature animal will develop out of a baby one, but we can never know what will become of a human being. Human souls are not fixed in their power to change. They can die and be born again many times over. The changes caused by nature, great as they are in the human constitution, are only a beginning. The transformations wrought by the human spirit are without limit. If Faust had stopped changing, if he had been unwilling to go on dying and being born in soul, he would have come to the point of denying the human spirit, of driving out the great changing force within himself. The Devil would have kept him then, for he would have ceased to be a true human being. This vital point — the decision to change or remain fixed — is the crux not only of Goethe's *Faust* but of the drama of every human life. The question of human life is not 'to be or not to be' — that falls too short; it is the further question: 'to become or not to become?' To answer 'become' is to say yes to the incompleteness of human life and to say yes to the spirit in the human being. The sacraments have a place in human life because of its unfinished character, and because every human being has a power to become, to grow towards the Spirit. The sacraments are deeds that on the one hand complete the natural events of life by the grace of the

Spirit, and on the other foster the inner growth of the soul towards its fulfilment.

The seven sacraments which are celebrated in The Christian Community follow the course of a human life-time, joining to that which comes about by nature that which is done through the working of Christ. By the natural event of birth, the child is received by its parents into the family. To this is added the sacrament of Baptism through which the eternal spirit of the child is received by the community of Christian people on earth. Beyond family, nationality and circumstances is that part of the child's being which existed before birth and is now called into earth existence in the name of Christ.

The natural event of growing-up, the birth of the soul at the age of puberty, has its spiritual counterpart in the sacrament of Confirmation. Up to this moment children have been shown the picture of Christ outside of them. From now on they will have the power of soul to search within themselves for the presence of Christ.

In adult life there are two sacraments that accompany us day by day. The one is the sacrament of Communion, the Act of Consecration of Man. One part of our human nature depends on earthly food, and can die of starvation, but another part is hungry for the spiritual food of God and grows feeble if it is not nourished. Our bodies need daily food and our souls seek to be fed by the words in which the spirit of Christ speaks and acts. The second is the Sacramental Consultation. We all carry about with us our load of cares, problems and responsibilities. These burdens can be brought into the presence of Christ and carried away again in fresh understanding and strength.

Two other sacraments belong to the decisive turning points of a lifetime. The first is the Sacrament of Marriage. In ordinary life this is a natural event in which the natural human urge to unite what has become separated and one-sided in man and woman is at work. But this union is also a festival in which the spiritual selves of the two personalities show their will. The sacrament expresses what is being said by their spirits and by the spirit of Christ, which will endure beyond the moment when the natural forces of attraction come to an end. The other is the Sacrament of Ordination for priests. The sacraments need people to celebrate them. For this purpose a spiritual substance must be added to those powers which human beings can develop out of themselves. Each one who undertakes to become a celebrant passes through Ordination into the priesthood.

The last of the sacraments is there for the last great event of a lifetime, death. The power of nature that builds up our bodies also dissolves them. The soul and spirit must leave and return to the world from which they came forth. In the Anointing the soul is led out of the dying body to the gate of death. Christ is the companion on the way over the threshold between two worlds and two forms of existence.

The sacraments express what the grace of Christ offers to human souls. Through him the power to become streams into us. He is the pattern of our fulfilment. He works in the unfinishedness of our selves, our life, our world. The sacraments are his words and deeds present with us, helping us to 'be perfect,' as he urges us (Matt.5:48).

Sacramental working

Before we turn to the detailed description of the sacraments themselves as they are celebrated in The Christian Community, we should describe briefly a view of the world which has space for something like the sacraments. We might put this as a question, namely: how can we think of the sacraments as something important and real when we know that the world works according to predictable, physical laws?

As much as individual human beings never cease to change, humanity as a whole is undergoing a development in which human beings have gradually freed themselves from external authority and, mainly through their thinking, sought to attain independence. It is part of the situation of our time that the power of the human intellect, which has been such a help on the journey of the human being towards autonomy and responsibility, has created a view of the world that has no place for the essential nature of the human being, which is spiritual, nor for any spiritual view of the world. It is even the case that most theologians base their methods of research on the assumptions of materialistic science. Often it seems that faith is something quite subjective, a little corner in the human soul besieged by the forces which govern the world around.

It is in the light of this development which started at the time of the Renaissance and has reached its height since the Enlightenment, that we can see the changing attitude towards the sacraments. If faith is understood as a purely subjective concern of the human heart which has no relationship to the world of 'objective reality,' then sacraments can be no more than symbols, more or less arbitrary signs which help to strengthen our faith. Thus it is that, particularly in the Protestant Churches, the emphasis has moved away from the sacraments as magical acts to the individual relationship of the believer to God. Even the sacraments in The Christian Community can be viewed in this way, but this would not do justice to their essential nature. They imply a different view of the world than a materialistic one. They imply that there is an objective world of spiritual reality that stands behind and beyond the phenomena of our world. It is not an 'otherworldly' view, however, for the world of spirit is the origin and source of our world, and the two worlds are in essence a unity. The substances of the earthly world can be reunited with their spiritual source, as in the Sacrament of Baptism. They can become bearers of the transformed earthly world that Christ wrests from the forces of death to become the future earth, as in the Act of Consecration of Man.

There is another question that should be addressed, which is particularly relevant to those parts of the world with a Protestant heritage. We have mentioned how the idea of the role of priests that made them into magical mediators between human beings and their God is rejected by the Protestant Churches. This rejection was part of the great spiritual revolution that took place at the time of the Reformation. It would be easy to see a Church which takes seriously the objective working of the sacraments as a return to a medieval form of Church life which denies the spiritual freedom of the faithful and makes them mere passive recipients of sacramental grace. It is here that the sacraments of The Christian Community contain something quite revolutionary, a new conception of the congregation that allows both for the objectivity of the sacraments and the need for the subjective involvement of those who wish to participate in them. Thus the Communion service, the Act of Consecration of Man, begins with an invitation to all who are present worthily to fulfil it; it ends with the simple assertion that it 'has been.'

The key to understanding this seeming paradox is the idea of the angel or spirit of the congregation. We learn from the Revelation to St John, Chapters 3 and 4, that every church, every congregation has an angel. Members of a congregation are called upon to enter into a relationship with this angel, and to bring their own strength to help the angel in his task. Without the congregation there cannot be Christian community; yet the effectiveness of the sacraments does not only depend on the spiritual strength of individual members. It is a case of the whole being greater than the sum of its parts. As a *community* we are able to do far more, to go on a spiritual path far greater, than we are yet able to do as individuals. But it is no longer the case that we are unable to go any distance at all, and must wait patiently for the priest to bring us the spiritual substance we need.

The Christian Community

In The Christian Community seven sacraments are celebrated: Baptism, Confirmation, Communion, which bears
the title: The Act of Consecration of Man, Sacramental
Consultation, Anointing, Marriage and the Ordination of
Priests. They accompany the human being on the path
through life from birth to death. In this sense these sacraments have been known from the first beginning of
Christianity. Since the Reformation there are parts of the
Christian Church which recognize sacraments, but accept
only two (Baptism and Communion).

The Christian Community was founded in 1922 as a
movement for the renewal of Christianity. The founders
were inspired by concern about the cleft that had formed
between the Christian Churches existing at that time and
the new form of consciousness that is being born in human
souls in the twentieth century. They were aware of the
danger that religion would come to be seen as a purely
inward, subjective concern of the human soul in a world
that had no space for spiritual reality or God. The cleft is
clearly expressed, for instance, in the difference between
'Church' language, beautiful but old-fashioned, and the
language in which modern people strive to express their
thoughts. The founders were able to put their concern into
action with the help of Rudolf Steiner. His Anthroposophy
or science of the spirit provides the foundation for a world
view that has space for an objective working of the sacraments. The Christian Community was not founded for any
one country, though the actual foundation meeting was held

in Switzerland, and its work began there and in Germany. Today it is at work in Northern and Central Europe, North and South America, South Africa, Australasia and beginning in Eastern Europe and Japan.

A new Church cannot be only man-made, however good the will of its would-be founders. A new revelation was able to flow from the spiritual world, giving The Christian Community its spiritual substance and its power to exist. The spiritual Sower went forth to sow and cast a new seed on the earth. The seven sacraments are this seed. There is no question that they are new in themselves. The sacraments emerged in the course of the early history of Christianity, but the past forms of their expression have grown old and remote for the reasons that we have discussed above. The sacraments of The Christian Community are their new expression in the present age with its new consciousness. They are in this sense both old and new. It is the same Sower who goes forth to sow the Word of God, but time goes on, and for the new season the new seed is sown.

This statement simply expresses what those who believe in The Christian Community would say about their own Church. Everyone can test its truth by attending one of the services where anyone who wishes to come is welcome. The Christian Community does not wish to make claims, but to say: Come and see for yourself.

There is no Prayer Book in The Christian Community. The texts of the rituals are not published in printed form nor read in books by members of the congregation. This is so because the services are there to be heard and experienced. Theirs are not written but spoken words. Although this seems foreign to our age in which everything important is printed, it can be experienced as a great gift. Being able only to hear, not to read the words, means that one's relationship to them is not intellectual or analytical. One listens in quite a different way to words one has not read. This listening of the congregation is safeguarded in The Christian Community with every care. The descriptions of the services which are to follow are intended as a guide and introduction to those who wish to attend them or who have begun to do so and would like some help in finding their own way into them. For these reasons the wording is not quoted, but what happens is described. The seven descriptions are be organized in the form of answers to four questions:

> Who takes part?
> What is used?
> What is done?
> What happens?

Baptism

Who takes part?

The child; the parents; the congregation; the godparents; the priest

THE CHILD

Baptism is the sacrament that is the spiritual counterpart to birth and the beginning of life. In it the child is welcomed into the community of Christians which undertakes to guide and nurture it in the coming years. It is given to the child soon after it is born. Being born is a dramatic event in human existence, and new-born babies show many signs of the struggle they are going through. In birth a human soul comes down from the spiritual to the earthly world. Birth begins when the child leaves the shelter of its mother's body, but this moment only marks the beginning of a long process that lasts in reality until the child has become an adult. The struggles that can be witnessed going on in the small body in the first weeks are overcome and later a healthy baby grows to look settled and comfortable on the earth. But one kind of struggle has only been exchanged for another: the effort to sit up, to get teeth, to form sounds and words begins, and when this is over still another kind starts. Being born and growing up mean struggle and labour all along the way and every successful struggle brings the joy of something accomplished. How little children who have just succeeded in walking on their own two feet can laugh!

But children need help in the struggle to be born and this is given to them by the Sacrament of Baptism as early as possible. The spiritual act has a direct effect on the constitution of the child's soft, unfinished body, on the strength of the soul to unite with it and on the power of the spirit to enter the world of earth. When we then ask: who takes part in a Baptism, and the first answer is: the child, this means the child in body, soul and spirit, as they all struggle to be born.

Baptism in The Christian Community is a gift to the child. The words of the service are distinctly addressed to a human soul seeking its way down to earth. This is something new in the history of the Christian sacraments. The older forms of Baptism come down from the first centuries of Christianity when the predominant practice was the baptism of adults, as it was in New Testament times. Gradually these forms were adopted for infants born into Christian families. For this reason elements such as vows to renounce the world, the flesh and the devil, all of which assume the conscious presence of the one who is baptized, are still part of many baptism ceremonies. As new-born children cannot make vows, it became the custom for the godparents to make them on their behalf.

The form of service in The Christian Community is new in that it is meant specifically for children up to the age of fourteen when they are confirmed. Its intention is to initiate them in a Christian sense into life on earth. It is not the custom to use it for adults who were not baptized as children. The Greek verb from which our word 'Baptism' comes means 'to dip.' Baptism means to dip or plunge into the stream of sacramental working. In conscious participation in the Act of Consecration of Man this is what can happen. In this sense the Act of Consecration of Man contains a baptism.

The child has been described as 'the soul seeking its way down to earth.' This picture is given by the service itself, the wording of which implies a definite idea of what it means to be born. This idea may be put into words in the following way. The human body is built up throughout the months between conception and birth by a complicated process of development. After birth it goes through a still longer process of growth and unfolding before its maturity is reached. The body is full of wonders; the greatest wonder of all is that it is a house which an invisible inhabitant is building as its own dwelling place. The body is the living house of the soul which lives on earth not only *in* this house but *with* it and *through* it. The eyes are not only windows, they are more, they give the soul sight. The hands and feet give the soul the opportunity to move and to act. The body is a house, but a magical one that lives and moves as long as the inhabitant is at home.

To the question whether human existence begins at birth or before, we can answer that the body begins to exist at conception, but the soul has lived before. The inhabitant was there long before the house, for the soul itself was the builder, aided by others. The soul has lived before birth in the world of spirit. It bears within it the eternal self (or individuality) of the human being which is by its nature a spirit among spirits. This part of every human being has its home in the spiritual world, but its place of work is on the earth. It has therefore to seek incarnation or the life in the body. It has to descend from the heights of spirit to depths of earth. For the child's body growing older is growing *up*; for the spirit and soul it is growing *down*. Behind the helpless little body that is in need of care for so long is the full grown self, with all that it knows and cannot say. The words spoken in the Baptism service are said, as it were, across the tiny body to the great being of spirit who stands above and behind. The child is addressed in his or her threefold nature of body, soul and spirit.

THE PARENTS

Baptism is celebrated in The Christian Community for the sake of the child. In many other Churches today the stress is now being laid on the part of the parents in the service, as it is felt to be easier to address the grown-up people than the unconscious baby. There is a true story of a clergyman holding this view, who had a crying baby removed into the vestry during the Christening because, he said, its cries interrupted his exhortations to the parents. But there is a higher level of consciousness than the one where exhortations are received, on which the little child is aware of the act of Baptism. For the child's later life it will be one of the deep unconscious memories which according to psychological evidence affect our minds more than things remembered. The baptism is for the child but the parents have chosen to bring their child to the altar. One of them holds the child in their arms throughout. This fact expresses eloquently what the parents signify at this moment. They have opened their arms to receive the helpless, unfinished little being who finds through them the way to a life on earth. They give warmth, food, a home and loving care though the years of struggle to become adult. They make a place in the world for the child who has come to them, surround it with a family, whose name it receives, give it a nationality and teach it a mother tongue.

It is quite common nowadays for parents to talk as if it is they who decide whether they want a child and when.

However, in so doing they leave out the other, more hidden side of the matter; they overlook the wish of the unborn child to come to them. Guided by the divine wisdom of the world in which they live before birth, children choose the parents who will give them the kind of heredity and surroundings which will fit them for life on earth. They seek their fathers and mothers with such strong loving trust that they put themselves as helpless little babies into their hands. Before the parents have had time to love them, they have approached them with their own love. All this is expressed in the Sacrament of Baptism, not in words, but in the picture which is made when one of the parents carries the child in their arms to the altar.

By bringing their child to the Sacrament of Baptism in The Christian Community, the parents show their intention of bringing the child up in a way which continues what the Sacrament of Baptism inaugurates: their life in the community of Christians on earth.

THE CONGREGATION

All those who are present at a Baptism are called on actively to take part. They are addressed directly as the 'dear' congregation. They have come together in the name of Christ that the child may be received 'into the communion of the Christ Jesus.' The child has already been received by its very birth into one earthly community, the family. However, there is a part of every child, of every adult too, which is not of the family. It is the individual soul which bears within it that to which in the truest sense each of us can say 'I.' In token of this, each of us has a Christian name as well as a family name. The Christian name is solemnly spoken in the Baptism in front of all the community of Christians. We owe it to the working of

Christ in our earthly life that we can all be aware of the true individuality within ourselves, and can recognize it in other people. Without Christ we could not do this. Only in the name of Christ therefore can people come together to receive into their midst this part of a child's being, as he begins his earthly life. The community has a task too in the Christian upbringing of the child, even if this is indirect, taking the form of support for the life of the congregation, so that the baptized children can experience Christian community as a place where they receive nourishment and help during their upbringing.

The spirit of freedom in The Christian Community means that parents are sometimes unclear about what is meant by baptism *into* the community. Baptized infants are not included in a register of members — membership in The Christian Community is a conscious act of an adult human being. Neither has it been the custom to expect that parents become members before bringing their child to baptism. On the other hand baptism in The Christian Community is not baptism into nothing. Christianity is not merely an idea about which we tell our children, but it has a body, both in the person of Christ and in his Church. Baptism leads the child into a relationship with this body, and charges the adults to lead the child to grow more and more part of it. We do ourselves, the sacrament and our children an injustice if we make the Sacrament of Baptism into a matter of empty convention. Even if the parents are not members, they will wish to be in a relationship with The Christian Community and their local congregation.

In the final prayer the celebrant states that he or she has celebrated the Sacrament of Baptism 'before and with' those who are present. In these words is made clear that in the sacramental life of The Christian Community, there can be no question that the congregation watches passively whilst the priest performs sacramental 'magic' in front of them. The members of the congregation are called upon actively to participate in the sacrament through their presence, and above all to foster the working of the Baptism in the soul life of the child during the ensuing years.

THE GODPARENTS

Just as the parents are the two posts of the door through which the child enters the community of family and nation, so the godparents are the door posts to the community of Christians. The two godparents sit on either side of the parents during the service. Their names are spoken in front of the congregation and each is acknowledged by the celebrant taking his or her hand as a sign of the promise they are making. They do not actually speak, but the celebrant speaks to them words that are a task. They are charged to lead the child's soul in the community of Christ. Nothing is said about training or education, but 'leading.' This means 'going with,' and 'going in front' to show the way.

The first part of the godparents' task is to show, through what is Christian in themselves, the way to become a Christian among Christians. Children and young people are far more likely to be impressed by qualities embodied by people they respect and love, than by ideas they try to tell them about. The godparents are to lead; the child is left free to follow him or herself. The power, out of which they are able to undertake so much, is described in the words of the service as the heart's sacrifice. To open one's heart and to take into it another human soul to whom one is not bound by natural ties and to carry this other destiny with

watchful care is an act of sacrifice. At this moment the joy
that the godparent naturally will have in the relationship,
the pleasure of watching the child grow and develop is in
the background. The solemn responsibility is in the fore-
ground. In the German text of the Sacrament of Baptism,
the godparents are referred to as *die Wächter*, the watchers
or guardians. They watch over their godchild, as helpers of
the growing soul, as hinderers of everything that might
prevent the godchild from reaching the purposes of spirit
with which it came down to earth. They should be persons
of trust in the family whose advice will be welcome in all
that concerns the child's welfare.

The godparents' task has another dimension. A task of
Christian leadership is more than a purely human relationship. It will acknowledge the unfinished nature of a human
life that we described in the Prologue, and the need for
help that goes beyond what human beings can achieve
alone. The source of such leadership is in intercessory
prayer. Many people today find it hard to pray. As modern
human beings we can no longer pray simply because we
are told to. However, to cultivate one's own relationship to
prayer can be a source of great strength; and even if one
cannot do this for oneself, to do it for another person, a
godchild or the married couple to whom one is the witness,
is truly a Christian deed.

Awareness of the nature of the godparents' task can be
a help for parents in choosing people to be godparents.
Parents tend to look amongst their friends and family for
the godparents; it is natural to look in the circle of people
who are close to the family. However, there are criteria that
go beyond this. The godparents take on their task on behalf
of the congregation. Even if they are not members they will
need to be open to the idea of The Christian Community
and to identify with its aims. They must be prepared to

make a sacrifice. And they must be open to taking on a Christian task of leadership that involves prayer.

No relationship is so free as that of godparents to the godchild. Parents choose their children much less than the children choose them. But godparents choose out of their own free will to open their hearts and take in this special child. They have none of the unavoidable duties of parents but they have opportunities to help. And the growing child will look back and feel: these friends, who had no duty to me, have been of their own will following the steps of my life with love and prayerful care in the name of Christ.

THE PRIEST

The Sacrament of Baptism begins with a prayer spoken to the 'Spirits of Worlds.' The one who celebrates the ritual has to turn first of all to the worlds of spirit from which the soul of the child is descending and pray to divine beings who are guiding them to earth. In birth there is a shadow of death and in death there is the gleam of life. These guardian beings let human souls as it were die away from them into earth existence. They follow their ways on earth with care but from a distance. One day, when their time is served, they will call them home again. To them the celebrant turns first and then to the gathering of Christian people who are waiting to receive the new-born soul. The celebrant stands during the Baptism on the threshold between two communities; the community of spirit from which the soul is coming, and the community of earth into which the soul is entering. The priest's task is to lead the child into the community of Christians on earth.

What is used?

The vestments worn by the celebrant for Baptism are a long purple cassock, over it a shorter white alb and a purple stole.

In front of the altar a small table is placed with two cloths, a blue one underneath, a red one on top. The two colours are to each other what the sunlight is in the blue sky. The blue of the sky stretches into the distances and enfolds the world. From the fiery point of the sun's ball, the light radiates. Two aspects of the Godhead are expressed in the picture they make, the same are expressed again in the colours blue and red. On this table three vessels are placed containing water, salt and wood ash. The child is baptized with these three substances.

Water is the substance that brings life into the earth. Where there is not enough water the ground is unfruitful. When water falls on the dry seed, it begins to swell and to sprout. When it rains the plants grow larger and greener. Salt is the substance that gives form, that holds in shape, that crystallizes and preserves. The process embodied by the salt complements that of the water. Ash is the substance left over when the fire has burnt out. It is as dead as matter can be. But it is one of the mysteries of the earth that new life, that is to say new spirit, can only take hold of earthly matter and transform it when matter has first gone through a kind of death. The seeds of the plants are nothing else than little grains of ash left over when the plant has burnt itself out in the sun's fire. What happens when ash and water and salt come together? The forces released from these substances work together for growth, for spirit becoming matter. The child is baptized with the three substances which, when the forces in them are released, work together for growth.

What is done?

The service of Baptism falls of itself into seven parts or stages, according to those to whom it is addressed. The first prayer is spoken to the spirits of worlds who lead the child's soul through the gate of birth. The celebrant states clearly the intention of the Sacrament of Baptism which is to lead the child into the community of Christians on earth.

The second part is spoken to the community of Christian people who are present. Their task is described: they are to receive the child and carry him or her into the community.

In the third part the godparents rise on behalf of this community, their names are said, the celebrant shakes the hand of each and speaks the charge of leadership to them.

The fourth part is spoken to the child. The celebrant gives the child its Christian names in the power of Christ.

The fifth part is the baptism with the substances. The celebrant takes each substance in turn and speaks the words of consecration over it. In these words the substances are reunited with the spiritual processes that they embody. Each substance becomes the vessel for a spiritual force. An aspect of birth is the encounter with the unyielding, hard substance of earth. In the Sacrament of Baptism children encounter earthly substance that has become transparent for the spirit. The celebrant applies a small amount of the consecrated substance to the child and makes a sign on the child's head; with the water, a triangle on the forehead; with the salt, a square on the chin; with the ash, a cross on the chest. The child is charged to live in the community through the power of the consecrated substances. After this the child is blessed in the name of the Trinity.

In the sixth part the community of Christians is addressed as those who have celebrated the sacrament with the priest. They are reminded of the task of leadership that they have taken on by their presence in the Baptism.

Finally, the celebrant speaks the Lord's Prayer to the Father in the heavens.

It is the custom to begin and end the service with music. In The Christian Community music is felt to be capable of giving its own expression to the revelation of Christ. However, much work has still to be done towards discovering how different instruments and compositions best meet the different occasions in the life of the sacraments.

What happens?

In order to attempt an answer to this question we must imagine that our eyes were different and could see not only what is, as our present eyes can, but what exists as potential, what is yet to develop. We go into a garden that is being planted in the spring. There are two flower beds that have been prepared for sowing: the soil is clear of weeds, the surface has been neatly raked and firmed down. For normal human eyes there is no difference between the two. But when we look at the one bed we see floating above it the hazy forms of the flowers that will grow there, whilst above the other we see nothing. The first bed has been sowed, the second has not. Something has changed objectively, yet the change is almost entirely one of potential.

The Sacrament of Baptism refers to objective processes taking place. The priest names the child, and baptizes him or her three times with the consecrated substances. On the other hand the Sacrament of Baptism states repeatedly that its intention is to 'lead' the soul into the community.

Baptism is actually about a relationship to a community. This is something that can only grow over time.

What kind of community is it, into which the child is led? It is a sacramental one. It is not by chance that the Sacrament of Baptism takes place in the church, in the same space where the Act of Consecration of Man takes place, as far a possible amongst the members of the congregation who attend the Act of Consecration of Man. This community is uniquely able to understand and feel responsible for what has been inaugurated through the Sacrament of Baptism, the objective change that is almost entirely potential. For this reason, the question 'What happens?' is hardly adequate. We should rather ask, 'What has begun that is yet to come?' This way of talking is familiar to us from the New Testament, where Christ refers to himself as the one 'who is and who was and who is to come' (Rev.1:8). His kingdom is both a present reality, and something that has still to be revealed.

We can see the Sacrament of Baptism too as a new birth. The child's body has been born already in the course of nature. Now by the spiritual act of Baptism the soul is born through the working of Christ. The two births are recognized in the custom that we each have a 'surname' or family name, into which we have come by the first birth, and 'Christian names,' which are chosen for us and given at the Christening or baptism. It is not easy to choose the right name. It should belong to us personally and express something of what is hidden within us. The father of John the Baptist heard his name from an angel. The angels are indeed those who best know what our proper Christian names are and they have their own way of dropping us hints if we are able to notice. The best preparation for a good choice is to realize what Christian names mean. To name children after their uncles, aunts and other relatives is to confuse the Christian name with the surname.

The child is born into the community of Christ. This does not imply that the child is thereby made a member of The Christian Community as a Church in earthly form. All Christian people, to whatever Church they belong, are part of the community in the sense of the baptismal service. The Christian Community is able to give Baptism to any child whose parents ask for it in good faith, without making any claims. All the care and help that a Church can give will be given to children baptized in the community in their growing years but they will still be able to make a free decision as adults about which Church or religion they wish to join. To be received into the community of Christ is not the same as becoming a member of a particular church. We might try to understand it with the following image: The soul of the child has left the community of spirit and finds itself on earth where human beings are separate from each other. In Baptism it is received into a community of Christians as if into a womb. In Confirmation this relationship changes, as we shall see below. Finally, in becoming a member, the relationship has been transformed completely and members are concerned to create the 'womb' in which newcomers can be nurtured.

The child is born into the community with the earth. In the water, salt and ash the forces are consecrated through which the soul can work on the growing body. Baptism changes the way in which the soul grows into its earthly house. When the earth first came into existence it was the house of God and its nature was divine. Then the separation between the divine world and the world of earth happened which is called in the Bible 'the Fall of Man' because it came about through human beings. Now every soul is born into a body that shares in the fallen, sick nature of the earth. To grow up means, from one side, growing aware of the sickness in the world around and in one's own nature. But in the Baptism the child's soul meets the forces of bodily growth restored by the words of consecration to the divine, pure form that they had at the creation of the earth. Before the child has become aware of the sickness of earth they receive the healing power that works through Christ.

Confirmation

Who takes part?

The young people; parents, congregation and priest

THE YOUNG PEOPLE

The sacrament of Confirmation is given in The Christian Community to boys and girls at the age of fourteen. It marks the most dramatic change in the long process of growing up, the one which is usually covered by the word 'puberty.' It is the time of life when childhood ends and youth begins. At the beginning of the Confirmation service the young people are received with the words 'Dear children,' but as the service proceeds they experience they are becoming more than children.

What does it mean to change from a child into a youth? In the Prologue we described the process of growing up as being born twice. The body is born at the beginning of life, but the soul is born into independent existence at the end of childhood. That is how we can tell the difference between a child and a youth. The individuality of children still hovers above them. Children often show strong signs of personality, but this is a shadow thrown from outside. The substance is not yet born; this is why young children cannot develop in a healthy way without experiencing authority. This does not mean that they should not have a will of their own and a chance to use it, but that they should be able to look to grown-up people, whom they love, to parents, to teachers and to others also, for guidance and decisions. 'Must I always do whatever I like?' is the way one little girl once expressed the pain of children who are forced to take responsibility for themselves. They cannot but feel pain when they are required to make decisions of which they are not yet capable. Take the simple example of a child who is making something and grows tired of it before it is finished. An adult sees the dilemma and helps the child to go on with it with enough conviction and firmness that it gets finished in the end. Children grow stronger when they can see what they have accomplished.

In such examples one can observe how different a being is the child from the grown-up person. And the essence of the difference is in this, that the children are surrounded by a kind of soul womb, woven of their own forces, of that which they receive from parents, teachers and friends, and of the forces of the cosmic world which still bears them up. But the adult has been born in soul as well as body and has an inner life of thinking, feeling and willing guided from within by the self. Once it is clear how wide the difference is between child and adult, the change from childhood to youth can be seen in its true importance.

As Baptism is given to children at the beginning of their life in the body, so Confirmation is given when the young people are beginning their own life of soul. From fourteen onwards all the grown-up powers of thought, all the various kinds of feeling and all the force of will are growing within the young people. It is an awkward time of life for them and for the people round them. Just as a baby has to cry, kick and bump itself until it learns to speak with its mouth and walk on its feet, so the young souls have to try their strength and learn their powers. This does not happen

without bumps and growing pains. Just as a child likes to
try out strange ways of talking and walking or to dress up
in other people's clothes, so teenagers try out different
ways of thinking, feeling and behaving. In the teens it is
natural to want to keep this new-born, precious thing a
secret, to want to keep part of one's self to oneself, and it
is unavoidable to be on one's guard against anyone — even
the best-loved — reaching out to touch it. Selfhood, with
both its light and dark sides, develops in them. It is a time
that can cause their parents great concern. However, behind
the changing surface of their soul life they are hiding the
secret of the growing soul and out of it grows the power to
become self-responsible.

At this age of the soul birth the young human being
becomes ripe for the world. As the young people change in
their inner nature, so they wake up towards the world
around. They need to learn as much as they can, to do as
much as they can and to experience as much as they can.
Their natural interest in the world grows and it is the
greatest help they can have in enduring the inner upheavals
of this period in life. They begin to be aware that we all
have our own destiny in the world, that we all need to learn
to find our own way for ourselves. At the bottom of their
hearts they all feel at this time what an important,
thorough-going change is happening within them and how
much they have to discover and to face in the world as it
opens up around them. They find in the service of Confirmation this feeling acknowledged as it were from outside
their own heart, and they can feel themselves being
consecrated for the new life with its bright hopes and
shadowy fears.

PARENTS, CONGREGATION AND PRIEST

The decision to receive Confirmation should be made by parents and children together. The time in the child's life when parents make important decisions on their own authority is coming to an end, but the time when the young person will feel capable of making all decisions for him or herself is only just beginning. It is not easy at fourteen not to be swayed by shyness or by the longing to do the same as one's best friend, and it can be a great help to have one's deeper feelings understood and supported by an older person. The father, mother and the child, who are about to lose each other in the old relationship, can become aware in making this decision together of the deeply rooted trust between them. This may be a shining memory in the years to come when they have to find each other in a new relationship, perhaps through painful trial and error. Confirmation marks a great change in the life of the parents, just as it does in the child's life. Parents need at all times mobile minds but never quite so much as in these years. Their children whom they think they know so well can start to seem strangers to them.

But it only hinders children if their parents cannot help saying or even feeling: I wish you could be as you used to be. When the parents sit behind their sons and daughters at the Confirmation service and hear its words they may feel a fresh strength to let go the childhood of their children and to accept the uncertain ways of youth. At this moment they are ceasing to be parents and getting ready to be the friends of those who have been their children. Up until now they have been walking along the road of life in front of them, leading with their authority. Now they have to fall back and let them go on alone, finding their own way, becoming responsible for themselves. But parents and children can still walk together and the young people may often enough be glad to look round and find the protecting, watchful companions still near them.

The Godparents should also be present at the Confirmation. They are foremost among the 'people dear to you' who have been leading the way, about whom the words of the service speak to the young people. In The Christian Community godparents are understood to be watchers over the whole lifelong destiny of their godchildren. Their office does not cease as these grow up. It may happen, of course, that being so much older, one or other of the godparents comes to the end of their life long before the godchild. But loving relationships between people do not cease because one goes through death. Godparents, like parents, have to find a new relation to their godchildren with each age of life, but they remain the watchers in the spirit.

The Christian congregation is witness of the Confirmation. The words of the service are all addressed to the young people who are being confirmed, but they are spoken in the presence of the congregation. 'For where two or three are gathered in my name, there am I in the midst of them,' said Christ and his words describe what a Christian congregation is (Matt.18:20). The spirit of the Community is carried during the sacrament by the celebrating priest. With this spirit he consecrates the young people for life. But the spirit of the Community receives the presence of Christ. In his name and with his power, the priest consecrates the young people for life. In the words he speaks, in the acts he performs, there come together what the congregation brings from the earthly world and what the presence of Christ brings from the world of spirit.

What is used?

During the service the confirmands sit in front of the congregation before the altar. Facing them they see the celebrant in a long red vestment, the cassock, and over it the short white alb and the red stole. Red is the colour of Easter in The Christian Community. Confirmation is always celebrated on one of the forty days of Easter.

The service falls into two parts, the prayers of Confirmation, and the Communion service, the Act of Consecration of Man, in which the confirmands take part receiving communion for the first time.

For the Act of Consecration of Man different vestments are worn. The young people are able to watch the change being made and thereby they see in a picture what the service to which they are being admitted stands for. The red cassock is exchanged for a black one which is then entirely covered by a long white alb. Over these the stole and girdle are put, they are in the colour of the festival, that is red. Over them comes the chasuble, consisting of two panels, one at the back and one in front. It is red in colour with two figures stitched upon it in green. At the back the figure is U-shaped and open at the top, in the front it is a lemniscate, a figure 8.

These are the vestments which are always worn for the Act of Consecration of Man, the only variation being in the colour of stole, girdle and chasuble which changes with the festivals and seasons. They represent in a picture the nature of the human being in body, soul and spirit. The black cassock is the body of death, the part of us that is purely physical and which only becomes completely visible in a corpse. The white alb is the body of life which enlivens the physical body and makes it a possible dwelling-house for the soul. The coloured chasuble is the soul being. The figures on the Chasuble bear many interpretations: we might see in the 'U' form how the soul, living in the house of the body, opens itself in devotion to the world of spirit. In the other figure we can see how soul and spirit are united, and the forces from above and below flow into one another. The stole is the symbol of priesthood. The covering for the head completes the picture. It is a biretta in black with three corners, of which the one over the right side is longest. This is all placed in a picture before the eyes of the young people.

They hear also two kinds of speaking. The prayers of the Confirmation are ritual words, but among them is inserted a sermon for which the biretta is worn and in which the celebrant describes in his or her own words what this important moment means in the lives of the confirmands. Addresses or sermons are not held for children in The Christian Community, but here for the first time the young people are spoken to as thinkers, as souls ripe to grasp with the power of human thoughts the words and deeds of the sacrament.

At one moment in the Confirmation the celebrant lays his hands on the head of each confirmand. The sacraments are deeds celebrated through actions and gestures. With this holy touch on the head the deed of consecration is performed for these growing souls. At the end of the Act of Consecration of Man they receive the bread and the wine, and therewith the healing power of Christ, flowing throughout the being of Man in spirit, soul and body.

What is done?

Baptism and Confirmation in The Christian Community are both free gifts of the spirit, given by the congregation of Christians to young souls on their way into the life on earth. They are like the magic gifts, of which the fairy tales tell, given to the young man who sets off from home to seek his fortune. He often does not understand the gifts or forgets them until in the stress of his trials he finds through them just the decisive help he needs.

As at Baptism so at Confirmation no claim is made on the young people. They are young friends who are free to choose membership later on if they wish. Nor are they asked to make any confession of faith. The words of the service are spoken to them and they receive them. They hear in these words about the change in life through which they are passing, that it means leaving the authority of parents and teachers and coming into responsibility for themselves. Then they are told about Christ, about how they can look for his presence in their soul life and in their destiny. He is described to them as the One who overcame death to bring life of soul. A part of the seventeenth chapter of the Gospel of St John is read which is also read in the Anointing, the service for the dying.

Two realities open themselves to young people at this time of life which are hidden from children. These are death and the sickness of sin in human nature. There is always a tragic side to being human and the discovery of this throws a shadow over the thrill of growing up. But at the moment when the young souls make this discovery as their own inner experience, the words of the Confirmation service open to them still another reality, the presence of Christ dwelling within the human soul. As they discover the tragedy, the Comforter and Healer is shown to them. After they have heard the Gospel they are blessed in the name of Christ for their coming life. The sermon follows. They are then dismissed into life as human beings ripe for the earth and their first experience in the new epoch is the Act of Consecration of Man which now follows.

What happens?

In order to appreciate what happens through Confirmation
it is necessary to go back a step and see what the religious
experience of the children has been before this event. In
The Christian Community there is a service for children, to
which children can come from the time they start going to
school until they are confirmed at fourteen. The changing
of the teeth is the natural moment at which a child's school
education should begin, though nowadays this is not often
observed. Before that time the whole business of life is
growing into the body. So much is this so that the child
does not need religious experience in the form of a service
until later. The Children's Service is held before the same
altar at which the sacraments are celebrated and all its
words speak to the children about something which lies
ahead of them. They prepare them for what they will find
when later they go to the Act of Consecration of Man.
Childhood is in every sense the time of preparing to be
grown-up; it is quite in the nature of things that the service
should have this character. A Christian service for children
could not be otherwise; for children Christianity can only
be the promise of things to come. Much is talked among
Christian people about Christian education, as if it were
possible to make or educate children into Christians, but
there is a deep misunderstanding in all this. And in this
problem lies the heart of the question: What happens in
Confirmation?

To carry this question further involves a little thinking
in terms of the Trinity. Everything which exists, the natural
world, the plant and animal kingdoms, and human beings,
the 'children of men,' has its being in God the Father, the
Ground of all being. All little children feel this in their
hearts; in their prayers and in their service they find put

into words what they know of themselves without words. Just because they are so young and so near to the divine world they can worship God. All they need to be given are the right words.

Christ is the Son God who chose to unite himself with the destiny of mankind on the earth. He took on human form, lived a human life on earth and went through death on Golgotha. With the power of his resurrection he heals and renews the sick souls of men who, without him, must disintegrate. He is at the same time the pattern of that which human souls have still to become and the giver of the power of becoming. The mystery of Christ can only be approached with the ripe powers of thinking, feeling and willing of souls that have grown down to the earth. Before the birth of soul has taken place, Christ is there beside the little children, but they can only know him inasmuch as they see his picture reflected in the hearts of the adults around them. But at the time of Confirmation, the powers of soul are ripening in the young people, which will give them the means to know Christ within their own hearts. They have been able to know God the Father from the beginning of life, now they will be able to know the Son of God. Of course, while no amount of religious instruction can 'make' someone a Christian, the children need to be prepared for the Confirmation so that they have the possibility of understanding what is happening in the service. Such instruction is offered in the congregations of The Christian Community in the time between starting school and Confirmation. Its extent depends on local circumstances.

In the Children's Service the celebrant points to the picture of Christ over the altar and describes in the words of the ritual how he died and became alive in human hearts. In the Confirmation service the young people hear that Christ, whom their parents and teachers wished to show them, will be their companion through their life and the strength of their soul. They know of themselves that they are growing up and can learn and do more than they ever could before. They know too that there is death and the sickness of sin in others and in them. They stand at the threshold of their earthly life, eager to know what it will bring them. Now they hear that there is a spiritual mystery to be discovered on earth, that they may seek with their growing souls for him through whom death is overcome.

Not all of those who receive Confirmation grasp what they have experienced. Some realize more than others, but most feel that they will understand it better when they look back in later years. This is quite as it should be, because the point is not how much they understand, but how much has happened in them. We each have to find the way to realize the mystery of Christ in our own hearts. The purpose of Confirmation is to show to the children who are growing up the quest that lies before them for which they will now be ripe. It sends them out into life with the picture of Christ.

The Act of Consecration
of Man

Who takes part?

The congregation and priests

To be truly human is to understand that we are unfinished, that we are on a journey towards a perfection foreseen for us (see Prologue). To call ourselves human beings is not a right, it is a privilege; as Christians we might say that it is a grace conferred upon us by Christ who represents the ideal of humanity. He consecrates us to the rank of human beings. We cannot earn this privilege, yet we must do what we can to make possible Christ's work of consecration with in us. The idea of the Christian Church is that we can do this more effectively as a community than as individuals. The central service of the Christian Church is the Eucharist or Lord's Supper. In The Christian Community this receives a new name that reflects this view of the relationship between the human being and God: the Act of Consecration of Man.

The service is celebrated by a priest in the vestments that have been described in the chapter on Confirmation (p. 41). On the front of the chasuble worn by the priest is to be seen the sign of the lemniscate, the figure 8. The priest celebrates standing at the point where the two

parts meet, where the world of spirit and that of earth
touch. The words spoken and the actions performed are
not the property of the priest but are laid down by the
ritual. In token of this, the service is read from a book.
What the priest says and does at the altar is not personal
but expresses the will of the divine world. Two members
of the congregation who also wear vestments assist the
priest at the celebration. One stands on the right side to
carry the service book and make the responses on behalf
of the congregation. The other stands on the left side to
carry vestments and vessels as they are needed. More than
one priest may be present and may also assist in the
service. All who wear vestments are there not in a personal
capacity but to carry out sacred duties; the personality in
everyone is silent, that the divine words may be said and
heard.

The opening words of the Act of Consecration of Man
call upon the congregation to do far more than merely be
there and receive what is given from on high. The members
of the congregation are 'worthily' to 'fulfil' the sacrament
along with the priests. This inner participation — one might
even say, concelebration — is something new in the
development of the Christian sacraments. It too rests on the
mystery of community: each of us could easily feel daunted
by the task of helping the Act of Consecration of Man to
take place, but as Christian community, whose sum is
greater than the parts, we can achieve far more than
isolated individuals could. The congregation's participation
is expressed in something in the Act of Consecration of
Man that may at first seem strange. This is the fact that for
most of the service the priest's back is turned towards the
congregation. In the language of gesture this means that the
priest stands at the front of the congregation, performing
the sacrament together with it. If the priest were to face the

congregation, the gesture would express the fact that they present the congregation with the outcome of a process in which it is not involved.

What is used?

The Act of Consecration of Man is celebrated at an altar on which seven candles burn; a picture of Christ hangs above it. The altar is the threshold between the two worlds, the world of spirit and that of the earth. The candles burn for the congregation as a sign of the inner flames that burn in their souls towards the spirit. The picture is the sign that Christ is himself the door between the two worlds.

There is a difference between the altars of The Christian Community and those in other Churches which is expressed in the depiction of Christ. In The Christian Community the altar picture always represents him as the Risen One and this is so because the Act of Consecration of Man continues in its words and deeds the work of the Resurrection. The Crucifix calls on us to think of how Christ entered into suffering and death. Every altar above which a Crucifix hangs tells us that a sacramental act is celebrated here which continues that sacrifice. For a very long time the Christian sacraments have been celebrated beneath the Crucifix, but today a new epoch of Christianity is beginning. Christ not only descended into death, he overcame death and became the giver of life. The Cross is represented in the altar pictures of The Christian Community, but over it shines the glory of the Risen One clothed with light and the colours of the rainbow.

The altar is covered with a white cloth and a coloured frontal. The colour changes with the festival seasons to correspond with all the coloured parts in the vestments of priests and servers. The vestments and coverings used in

The Christian Community are undecorated. There is nothing to blur the significance of the simple shapes and colours. Each festival of the Church year has its own colour: for Advent deep blue, for Christmas white with pale violet, for Epiphany magenta, for Lent black, for Easter red with green, for Ascension red with gold, for Whitsuntide white with yellow, for St John's Tide white with yellow and for Michaelmas rose with light green. The colour used at the times between the festivals is lilac. The walls of the churches and chapels in The Christian Community are also coloured lilac. It is beyond the scope of this introduction to describe how the colours and the seasons are related. However, the essential idea is that there is a relationship between the colours we see outside and the life of soul. The soul lives in rhythms that are again related to those of the year with its seasons, which bring round in their course the festivals of the Church.

In the course of the service incense is used first to cense the chalice and then the four sides of the altar. The incense used in The Christian Community has a noticeably different scent from that used in other churches. It contains juniper berries in addition to the gums commonly found in incense, giving the scent a sharp tang. Incense has a twofold effect. It works on the sense of smell in the people who are present, and thereby helps to change their mood and state of consciousness. That is the reason why there is such widespread prejudice against it. However, whereas some kinds of incense do lull the mind, the kind used in The Christian Community, with its complement of bitter juniper, wakens it and helps the congregation into a mood at once reverent and concentrated.

The second effect is that of the smoke upon the words. The incense gum dissolves completely into smoke on the glowing charcoal. The smoke rises, curling and dispersing into the air, carrying the spoken words upwards as it goes. What the plants can give through their sweet gum unites with the words spoken by a human being to form prayers that rise from this world over the threshold of the altar into the worlds of spirit. By means of the incense the plants become our helpers at prayer.

The priest sets down upon the altar the chalice and the paten (the small plate on which the bread is placed), first covered, then unveiled for the Offering. Where circumstances allow they are made of gold and silver. Just as the plants are our helpers at prayer, so the metals make the vessels for the Offering. The bread is carried to the altar on the paten. Water and wine are prepared on a side table and are poured into the cup during the service. Bread and wine are consecrated by the holy words that are spoken, to become the bearers of Christ's spirit and the spiritual medicine for the community of Christians. They make manifest the power of Christ that can penetrate into the physical, material layer of existence and transform it. This transformation makes clear that Christ's power can work in the whole of our human nature, both in our consciousness and in the depths of our bodies, of which we are quite unaware.

In bread and wine we see a polarity in the external world which is an image of one within the human being, that of body and blood. Bread is made of corn, that is to say from plants that more than all others transform their substance into seed ripened in the sun. The corn stalks are empty when the ears are full. So are our bodies built up and fed by that which comes from above, penetrating that which comes from below.

Wine is made from grapes, that is to say from fruit that ripens in the sun after the summer has begun to wane. The fruit grows on a vine which sends into the earth longer roots than any other plant, but it must have a prop to grow upwards to the light. So our blood is created by that which comes from below, enlivened by that which comes from above. In the Communion the transformed bread and wine carry the power of consecration into the body and blood of men and women. They are consecrated by virtue of the fact that Christ has taken them for his body and his blood, and thereby the Earth herself also receives consecration.

What is done?

It should be stressed that the Act of Consecration of Man is, as its name says, an act and a process through which something happens. It has four parts which should be understood as four stages in the process. Outside these four main parts, which are the same whenever the service is held, a prayer that changes with the festivals of the seasons is spoken at the beginning and the end.

The Act of Consecration of Man is celebrated every day. How can we, with our modern minds which move so quickly from one thing to another, understand this act repeated daily in the same words? There is another divine act that happens every day the same but without the help of human beings. It is the rising, shining and setting of the sun without which our life would be impossible. We can think of the Act of Consecration of Man as a spiritual sunrise. It leads us out of the everyday world into the spiritual. Earthly time and space become transparent for another dimension of reality. The roof and walls of the church continue to give us quiet and shelter, but to our inner eyes they dissolve. The cosmos, with sun, moon and stars opens above us, and around us the whole earth spreads out, all creatures living and moving upon it and men and women receiving nourishment like the multitudes of the Five Thousand. An invisible congregation joins the visible one; the souls of those who have died are present and the hosts of heaven, the beings of the world beyond the threshold of the altar draw near. What is said and done in the ritual is an act on which the whole of creation waits, as the earth in the morning waits on the sunrise. The transformation is at work within those who are present. Their outer personality is outshone by the power of their spirit. The true form of humanity rises from the depths within them, and each can say of himself: I am a human being in the sight of God. But it is difficult to describe in ordinary language the perspective in which the sacrament should be seen. Much must be left to the experience of those taking part, where hearts will also know more than they have words to say.

The first stage in the holy act is the reading of the Gospel. There are two prayers of preparation, and for the second the chasuble is taken off. The prayers are said towards the altar, but to read the Gospel the celebrant turns to the congregation. This expresses the fact that he or she reads as the mouthpiece of Christ. The power in the words is not from the celebrant, but from Christ's presence within them. The congregation stands up to listen as a sign of reverence and also as a sign of uprightness in the spirit. The Gospel elevates men and women to the posture which is most truly human, the head raised towards the heavens, the feet standing firmly on the earth. To turn a common saying to another use: 'It makes men of us.'

After the Gospel is read the celebrant removes the stole and reads the Creed. The stole is the token of priesthood; by removing it the priest shows that the Creed is read by an individual, albeit one clad in the cassock and alb. The priest reads in the vestments in which he or she entered the church for Ordination (see p. 109) — as a Christian human being. The Creed is the only part of the service to be read

without the stole. It is the answer to the Gospel in the sense
that it responds to the Gospel given by the spirit of Christ
with a statement of the Christian faith in terms of human
thought. If the priest read it wearing the stole it would
imply that it was being read on behalf of everyone who is
present. However, members of The Christian Community
are free and responsible for their own thinking. The
celebrant reads as an individual before the congregation. It
is up to each of those present to make their own relationship to what is said. Between the Gospel and the Creed, a
sermon is often preached. For the sermon, the preacher
wears the stole, for they speak within their office in The
Christian Community. The preacher also wears the biretta.
The biretta has two meanings. On the one hand it symbolizes the priest's office and is worn when entering and
leaving the place where a sacrament is held. On the other
hand it emphasizes that what is said is spoken by an
individual, in their ordained capacity as a teacher, and does
not form part of the ritual text.*

The second stage is the Offertory. The celebrant resumes
the chasuble and uncovers the cup and paten, on which the
bread is lying, before this begins. The words of the Offertory are spoken first to God the Father, 'the Ground of the
World.' The opening words acknowledge the darker side of
human nature, the consequences of the 'sickness of sin' that
have flowed as soul-substance to the Father. In the second
prayer the highest forces of the human soul are brought to
him, uniting with the substances of wine and water that are
poured into the cup which is then raised in token of
offering. What has been offered in water and wine to the
Ground of the World is now brought in prayer to Christ.

---

*   In a congregation where there is normally only one priest, the sermon
    usually precedes the Act of Consecration of Man.

The third part is the Consecration or Transubstantiation. Its prayers are all spoken to the Father, the Ground of the World, in Christ and through him. The bread and the wine are offered that they may become, by the power of the Father, the body and the blood of Christ. One may feel that the presence of the divine spirit has worked in the ritual until now in the sphere of the soul. Now it goes a stage deeper and works in earthly substance. Yet this substance already contains within it the seed of Christ's life as a consequence of his deed on Golgotha. What is done now in the sacrament may be likened to the quickening of a seed that has been planted in the ground. The heavenly forces of rain, air and sun touch the seed, releasing its potential to grow up into the fruitful plant. The bread and wine are living seed; the power of the God the Father streams into them from the heavens to change them into that which in their potential already are.

The fourth part is the Communion. The celebrant and the members of the congregation receive the Christ-filled bread and wine in his name, and thereafter his blessing of peace. The prayers of this part are all spoken to Christ. The consecration of bread and wine has flowed from the grace of God the Father. Now Christ gives the consecration to the souls of men and women, healing them through the working of the Holy Spirit. When the Communion is given, those who wish to receive come and stand at the altar steps. They have stood up to hear the Gospel being read; standing, they receive Communion and blessing. The phrase was used earlier, 'the Gospel makes men of us,' to explain the point of standing upright when it is read. In this sense another can be used now and we can say, 'the Communion makes *new* men of us.' It gives us the strength not only to listen standing up, but to walk upright to receive Communion with Christ who consecrates us in body, soul and spirit.

The four parts are marked by the moving of the service book from one side of the altar to the other. For the Gospel reading the book is on the left, for the Offertory on the right, for the Consecration it is on the left in the centre, for the Communion on the right in the centre. These movements express in a detail the significance of the four stages of the Act of Consecration that have been described in outline. Left and right express the duality of human nature. The left is the passive or receptive side, the right is the active or giving one. From the left of the altar we receive the reading of the Gospel, which is given to us in the name of Christ. From the right side of the altar human souls may unite to bring the offering as if in answer to the gift of the Gospel. The book is on the left during the Consecration when the divine world answers the offering with the act of transformation, performed in bread and wine. Perhaps surprisingly, the book is on the right during Communion. This expresses the fact that to receive Communion is no merely passive act but an active union with the consecrated substance that Christ offers to us.

Each part of the service begins when the celebrant calls on the Trinity. In so doing he or she makes the sign of the cross: a long, downward stroke at the name of the Father, a cross stroke at the name of the Son, a circle round the cross at the name of the Holy Spirit. The members of the congregation answer with the sign of the cross in another form. Over the forehead, mouth and chin, and over the chest three small crosses are made at the names of the Father, the Son and the Holy Spirit. These crosses recall the places touched by the consecrated substances in the Baptism, and express the fact that every Act of Consecration of Man is a renewed 'dipping' into the stream of sacramental working. Each part of the Act of Consecration of Man ends with a greeting in the name of Christ from the priest at the altar to the congregation. The server speaks the answering words from the congregation to the priest. They are a prayer to Christ, that he may enter the spirit of the Community as it rests throughout the ritual on the celebrating priest. So through the words and deeds celebrated by the priest at the altar, the Act of Consecration is performed by the divine community of Father, Son and spirit within the community of Christians on earth.

What happens?

We have seen how the lemniscate or figure 8 on the chasuble symbolizes the fact that the Act of Consecration of Man takes place on the threshold between the world of earth and that of spirit. In attempting to answer the question 'What happens?' we shall see that much happens in each of these worlds that in turn flows into the other and influences it.

From the point of view of the congregation a process takes place whereby those who are present become the community of which we spoke in the Prologue: the bearer of the angel of the congregation. This process is described in the words of the Act of Consecration of Man. We enter the room in which it takes place as individuals. In larger congregations, we may not know our neighbours; we may even dislike them. However, as we participate together in the service, our higher self begins to unite with those around. After the Gospel reading, the server who holds the book for the priest responds, referring to 'our *soul,*' the single soul of the congregation that is elevated to Christ. In the third part of the Act of Consecration of Man, the priest refers to the 'loving *heart*' of the congregation; finally, before the holy moment of consecration, it is stated that the congregation 'knows' Christ. As individuals we might hesitate before claiming that we know Christ; as part of a community, we have trodden a path together that leads to this knowledge. We have recognized Christ's presence in heart and soul, and in the consecrated elements, the substance of the physical world.

All of this has an effect on us as individuals. Naturally the conscious experiences each individual has may be very different and may change from time to time. However, there is also this common experience: all those present come into the presence of Christ. No one can enter this presence without coming out again a changed person. Feelings about the world and oneself, one's point of view, aims and purposes go through a change. Moreover, something less conscious happens deeper still. In the presence of Christ we all find a part of ourselves that we cannot lay hold of alone, that we dimly know is there and long to find. It is the part of ourselves that is at home in the divine world which shines down like a star from above. Without always knowing it, we long for this divine child to be born in our hearts. Christ is the true 'pastor,' the Good Shepherd whose flock is made up of the higher nature of all human beings. Every time we encounter the Good Shepherd, he brings us closer to our true being. From Christ's presence flows out the magic of the soul's becoming.

On the other hand the Act of Consecration of Man is a deed for the earth and the entire cosmos that proceeds from Christ. A sacrament elevates the thoughts and feelings of those present; but beyond this it is a deed of the spirit with objective consequences in the world, which work on whether or not they are recognized by human beings. Christ's creative and transforming power goes out from the Act of Consecration of Man. In our description of the third part of this service, the idea of Transubstantiation was described very briefly. We shall now amplify that. To begin

with, in the three years of his ministry from the Baptism in
Jordan to the deed on Golgotha, Christ lived on earth as
God become man. What he did was different in its effect
on the earth, different from anything the greatest human
being could do, for in him God could work and create in
the form of Man. Most of all is this true of his death.
When his blood flowed from the Cross, when his body was
laid into the grave, this was the Communion for the living
being of the earth. The earth is just as much a living being
as men and women are, and it too has a living soul. It is
merely our present stage of consciousness that makes the
earth appear to us as something quite different from
ourselves. When people could speak, not with poetic
license, but seriously of 'Mother Earth,' they were nearer
to the truth.

When human beings die they part from the earth. The
mystery of the Resurrection is that Christ overcame death
and united himself with the life of the earth. Christ said to
his disciples, 'And lo, I am with you always, to the close
of the age,' that they should know that he is present in the
struggling, striving earthly course of humanity (Matt.28:20).
He works on earth and continues to work on earth, creating
into times to come. The work is begun but not finished,
and yet the aim and purpose are present in the ideal. This
thought helps us to reach the idea of Transubstantiation.
When bread and wine are brought to the altar they are the
fruit of the life of the earth, in which the power of Christ
has been at work since the deed on Golgotha. But they are
there like a seed that contains the living potential of a
plant. At the end of the world the whole earth is to be
transubstantiated into Christ's body and blood, not of a
sudden but as the fruit of a long transforming process. In
the Act of Consecration of Man the divine power of God
causes this promise for the future to be fulfilled on the

altar, and thereby the redeeming, life-giving process to be continued. The future of the earth and of humanity is created in the sacrament.

Human words and human actions in the ritual are the means whereby the work of new creation is done. The two worlds intermingle. Humanity is called upon to work with God. The Act of Consecration of Man, with its clear invitation that all who are present actively participate in this process, consecrates us not only in the sense that it bestows a special grace upon us. It consecrates us for a task: that we join in all humility in the working of the divine world on earth, fulfilling Christ's words when he spoke to his disciples: 'Tryly, truly, I say to you, he who believes in me will also do the works that I do; and greater works than these he will do, because I go to the Father' (John 14:12).

We have already mentioned the connection between the sacraments and the sun and the stars. Now this can be taken up again. As the outer sun is to the outer earth, so is the spirit of Christ to the living earth. As the sunrise is to the day, so the Act of Consecration of Man is for humanity and the world. When it is celebrated the spiritual sunrise dawns upon the natural sunrise. As human beings we can do nothing to make the natural sunrise; it gives us the daylight and we accept it as a natural fact. Of the other sunrise we are called to be helpers, we who are 'only human' are the fellow-workers of the Sun God.

Sacramental Consultation

Who takes part?

An individual and a priest

We can see the Sacramental Consultation as the sacrament
for the individual person, just as the Act of Consecration of
Man is the sacrament of the Community. There is a close
connection between the two. Both are repeated and can
accompany us through daily life, unlike the other sacraments which mark the great turning points of a lifetime.
When we go to the Act of Consecration of Man we do not
lose our personality, but we transcend the lower part of it
and find each our greater self. In the words of St Paul we
are present with the prayer 'it is no longer I who live, but
Christ who lives in me' (Gal.2:20). And in this sense we
find community with each other. But if we wish to come
into this mood of devotion and join in the immense task of
consecration that has been described, we must be able to
free our minds from anxieties, wishes and thoughts about
other things. This is not easy, for busy people, when they
sit quietly, tend to find all their problems coming to beset
them. It needs an act of will to put them aside. It is as if
we come into the church with a pack on our back, holding
all the hopes, fears and problems of our lives. But we need
to take the pack off, put it down by our side and forget it
until we leave again, finding that we have new strength to
carry it. If we can step back from the burdens we feel we

must carry, we may find that we can let some of them go — we have seen things out of proportion and are carrying a self-inflicted burden. Sometimes, on the other hand, we are chafing under the weight of burdens that we feel do not belong to us. How often do we say, 'If only I could get through this difficulty, then I would be able to get on with really important things!' With distance we can see that it is not only the great and noble things that belong to our burdens; there is value in everything with which we have to struggle. However, if we are to put down our packs we must be carrying them with a certain freedom and good will. The more irksome they are, the more difficult to lay aside. The purpose of the Sacramental Consultation is to help bring freedom in this part of human life.

Anyone who wishes for this help can go to a priest of The Christian Community and ask for it. No one has a duty to do so. Every member or friend of the Community is free to judge when he or she might need it. The meeting with the priest is private and it is not in itself necessary that it should take place in a church building. People who come to a priest may have reached a difficult patch in their lives; they may have an important decision to make; they may be concerned about something they have done; they may be in a situation beyond their control, where they have to act against their conscience; they may be threatened with some calamity, or they may have come to one of those high places on the journey through life from which it is easy and good to look back over the way one has come and to try to see where it is leading. These and many other moments there are, when the wish for this sacrament may arise. Very often people feel this wish when they are beset with troubles. This is natural enough, but the sacrament may be of great benefit in quieter moments when the whole pattern of a destiny can become clearer than in moments of stress.

There is no question in The Christian Community of a confession of sins. Those who wish to speak in such a Sacramental Consultation of things which are on their conscience are quite free to do so. Nevertheless, not only the shadow side of life, but every part of human destiny has its place in this sacrament. The priest undertakes to keep secret and confidential all that they are told, for what they hear they receive as a sacred trust, and not as information that interests them personally. The conversation with a priest is more than a conversation between friends. This does not mean that it should be without friendliness, on the contrary it should be full of warmth and confidence. But there is a danger associated with friendship, which only the best of friendships manages to avoid: that is, if we go to ask the advice of a friend, somewhere in our hearts we may expect to get an answer which 'is on our side.' We expect a kind of sympathy which takes our part against the world and our fellow human beings. Sometimes we frankly hope to hear the other person agree with us. But this is not so when we go to consult a priest within the sacrament. We see in the priest the representative of the divine world to which our own higher self belongs. We feel that both we and the one who is listening to us are seeking to meet consciously in the presence of Christ, that we are hoping to see together a part of destiny, as Christ himself may see it. The fact that the priest wears vestments expresses that this meeting is sacred.

What is used?

This sacrament has the form of a free conversation between the one who asks for it and the priest. At the conclusion ritual words of blessing are read, and the human words that have been spoken are answered by divine words. In this sacramental act words and only words are used. Nowadays the illusion is rather common that words are empty, hollow things. We say, 'Oh, it is all just words!' to dismiss something that has been said. It is true enough that many, many words are said, written and printed today that ring quite hollow. But this does not mean that all words are empty in themselves. If one begins to listen to other people talking and to notice how they speak rather than what they say, one can soon discover oneself listening through the words to the realm out of which the words are spoken. Some people's words have much greater weight than others, some sayings weigh heavier, because of the moment in which they are said. Some short remark may stick in one's memory and have an influence that lasts for years, while long speeches or conversations fade away and are forgotten.

Words have power; they are only empty when there is nothing behind them, when a lot of words are spoken where there is nothing to say. But we can all find examples in our own experience of words that have left their mark on us or on our lives; and they have made it either for better or worse. Words have an awesome power to destroy or to create, to help or to hinder, to make friends for us or enemies. But powerful though the effect of our words on other people, and theirs on us, may be, quite as powerful, if not more so, is the effect of our own words on ourselves. We change ourselves as we speak. Light and empty words make us weigh morally lighter; words filled with substance make us morally heavier.

This is not meant as a reproach against light talk in the sense of humorous or jolly conversation which can be a valuable balance to the serious side of life. What is meant here is that words we say with nothing behind them, with nothing of ourselves in them — whatever they are about —

alter our character a little and make it more trivial. But all the words which we can 'answer for,' those in which something of our selves speaks, they alter our character — whatever they may be about — by building up a substance within us. In Sacramental Consultation words are spoken seriously and responsibly. In ordinary life it is not easy to avoid a certain amount of empty talking. But in such solemn moments speaking has its true weight and importance, and those who have the courage to speak in this solemn, responsible fashion about their lives and about themselves become in so doing more responsible, morally stronger people.

What is done?

A Sacramental Consultation should be a proper conversation, that is to say a conversation with speaking and listening on both sides. But it should be a conversation with a purpose. It cannot be, for instance, the purpose of such a consultation that we have a chance to relieve our minds, or 'get something off our chest.' Afterwards our minds should be both relieved and strengthened, but not because we have had our say, but because the true purpose of the talk has been fulfilled. Nor is it the purpose that we come to the priest feeling that we cannot manage our life without help from someone else. No one needs to feel that to talk to a priest is an act of weakness; it is rather the case that the words of the Saint Paul are being fulfilled: 'Bear one another's burdens, and so fulfil the law of Christ' (Gal.6:2). Nor again is it the purpose that people come to such a consultation in order that the priest shall tell them exactly what they should do next, leaving them with the task of simply going and doing it. It is not the job of the priest in The Christian Community to tell people what they ought to do. But it is the proper task of the priest to try to help people to discover for themselves what is the right thing to do next, and even if they do the wrong thing, and do it again and again, to go on giving them spiritual understanding and care.

What then is the true purpose of this conversation? It is that the one who comes to the priest and receives the blessing should go away freer and more responsible than when he or she came. The key to understanding how this can be done through a sacrament is to be found in a secret about ourselves which is easily observed, but less often thought about. Throughout our lives we have to make decisions of varying degrees of importance. Some we make out of habit, without thinking at all. Others — sometimes important ones which we should really have thought out or at least made very conscious — we make according to what someone else we know would do at such a moment, according to what we were brought up to do and have done before, or even according to what 'is done,' or what 'is not done.' But some decisions we think out properly on their own merits, imagining various alternatives and what would follow from them. These last decisions are the only ones which we can truly be said to have made ourselves. These are the ones to which each one of us can say 'I.' In making them we have been able to feel responsible and free. Even if some of these decisions turn out less successful than those we have made according to custom or rule, this is less important than the fact that through them we could find ourselves as responsible people. The attitude to life that makes us avoid all risks prevents our growth as human beings. Out of this experience we can approach the much-discussed question of human freedom. It has long been a question for human beings, whether human freedom exists or not. Our experience with our decisions shows that the answer is not a simple yes or no. At some moments we are free, at others not. What then decides the difference? It is the question whether we are at a given moment truly ourselves or not; whether we are thinking and acting out of our true 'I,' or whether we are just 'jogging along' as usual.

Sometimes we are free and sometimes we are not. Is this just another of life's ups and downs? The answer to this is a plain no. Whether we are aware of it or not, there is a struggle going on within us that has both a personal and a cosmic dimension, that is, the struggle to become ever more free. Another way of describing it is as the struggle to become more and more our responsible true selves. We are still so much creatures of habit, of rules and regulations, of our education, of our family, of our nation, of our principles, and so little those selves who can think out an original, responsible decision, appropriate to the unique reality of the particular situation in which we find ourselves. What we have described as a struggle is in reality the throes of a great birth. All of us long in the depths of our hearts for this new birth of the spirit, through which we can become what in our innermost, hidden potential we are.

Sacramental Consultation is the sacrament that helps human souls in the birth of the true self, through which they can become responsible for themselves. Such a state-ment would be very much misunderstood if anyone should confuse the 'self' for which they become responsible with the shadow self, much better known to us in ordinary life, the self which we mean when we use the word 'selfish.' Here is meant by the term 'self' the part of us through which we become capable of self-sacrifice, the opposite of self-interest.

The sacrament can help in two ways. The conversation

between the priest and the one who comes to him aims at clearing the understanding. Human beings need to make sense of the world, but their thoughts are not always correct — often we explain things away because we cannot face them in their full reality. Nobody should be made to face something he or she is not yet ready to face; yet it is a problem when the partial explanations, the justifications and rationalizations become a part of our mental furniture. Then they act as a barrier to our truly understanding our situation. We cannot be free because we do not see our situation in its reality. The conversation with a priest can help us to 'clear out' old thoughts and make space for new thinking. We start to see our lives in ever wider perspectives — we see that there events come into our destiny for which the causes cannot be seen in one lifetime. Still others come in which are sent from the larger destiny of the world within which we have our own smaller one. The clearer the thinking about such matters becomes, the more the soul can practise the thinking in which the true self speaks.

Then there is the blessing at the end of the conversation. This gives the grace of Christ's strength to the struggling soul, that it may act as well as think with true responsibility for itself. Christ is our companion on the pathway of life, through trial and error, failure and achievement. This is expressed in this sacrament whose purpose it is to raise human souls to responsibility for themselves with the help of Christ.

In this sense it brings something new into the Christian sacraments. The sacrament for the individual person in the older Christian Churches had the purpose of taking away the burden of his or her own life. The Church, in giving absolution, took over much of the responsibility for himself from 'the son of the Church.' This was necessary as long as the spiritual birth of the true self could not yet take place. Today each person has at least the seed of self-responsibility because of the new birth of the true self. The Church must no longer take away responsibility but has the new task of giving it in the sacrament, and with it the strength to use it.

What happens?

The words of ritual spoken at the conclusion of a Sacramental Consultation have been described as a blessing. They are so in the sense that they are a contrast to the words of Absolution used in the older Churches. Absolution takes away, though the burden it takes away is dark. A blessing gives, adds new strength to what is already there. However, these words hold in them more than a blessing in this sense. The very first word of the Sacramental Consultation is 'learn.' In this word a world of reassurance lives. It tells us that Christ takes us seriously as pupils or, to use the Latin word, disciples. Whoever addresses us as pupils expresses the confidence that we can learn. Whatever errors we may have recognized in the conduct of our lives, we are standing not at the end of a process but at a beginning — we have the power to learn, to change.

The words of the sacrament show us how to perform an inner act, they show us what must happen within us, so that we can be open to receive the blessing of Christ. This is always the problem for human souls, not how to ask for spiritual help but how to be able to receive it.

In reality there is always more help at hand than we know how to take. People who believe that they have to bear all their troubles alone have not noticed what can really happen. For instance, we may find ourselves in a dilemma, or facing a difficult decision. We go to bed and lie awake worrying, inventing plan after plan, or fighting fear after fear. At last we fall asleep and awaken with a much clearer picture of the situation. Either then, or while we are dressing or a day later something occurs to us that we had never thought of, or we have a 'hunch' about what to do. In the thrill of anxiety relieved we may overlook how it all happened. If we look closer we will observe that the way out of our trouble has been sent to us. It did not come while we were worrying, but when we were not looking. While we were asleep a higher wisdom than our own was at work. But how difficult it is for the angels who are helping us, asleep and awake, to get in a word that we shall hear! That is how the words of this sacrament come to be so important. They tell us how to accept the help that Christ is always offering.

We have already described how easy it is for us to become attached to our thoughts, and how they can become an obstacle to our creative, living thinking. Even our ideas about positive things, our ideals, are in constant danger of becoming static. We like to hoard up the treasure of our mental world. The first thing we need to learn is to make an offering of our thoughts. This does not mean giving them up, or letting ourselves be over-persuaded by other people. It means that the thoughts should be offered to God. They should be lifted above the level of our opinions and wishes. They should be held up to the light of the divine world, for us to see how they look then. Certainly they will look different, the colours will change, perhaps the proportions and shape too. Perhaps one thought may become transparent for quite another one that was not visible before. Perhaps another thought may begin to reflect a quite different point of view.

In one way it is disquieting to watch one's familiar and even hard-won thoughts going through such changes. At the same time it is inspiring to see such a new, wide perspective, to see that some thoughts actually shine more vividly with wisdom than was to be expected. In the place of dead thoughts we start to experience living thinking. This is the first step of which the words tell us, but there is a second. They go on to instruct us to accept our will as a gift from God. Just where we usually make such efforts we should wait for what is trying to come to us. This is a second step and a consequence of the first. It does not mean that all that good people need to do is to sit and wait. It means that the new kind of thinking, which we attain through making the first step, has its own strength of will. It is already on its way to realizing itself on earth and we can go with it.

The verse goes on to describe how practising this twofold movement — the offering of thoughts and the acceptance of will — brings peace to our souls. It then describes the transformed relationship to the world that this exercise can bring about. The relationship to the world will be characterized by reverence for God; that to our fellow human beings will be characterized by love. The Sacramental Consultation helps us on our journey as Christians — it helps us towards our goal of living in constant awareness of God and in love of the world around.

Any notion that the Sacramental Consultation is concerned only with individuals is dispelled by this description of the new ideal relationship to the world. The purpose of the Sacramental Consultation is not to make us feel better — although to feel heard and taken seriously in the way that one is in the sacrament is a wonderful experience — its aim is to help us more fully to become free, responsible individuals, capable of life in true community with others. For this reason it would be false to contrast the Sacramental Consultation as the sacrament for individuals with the Act of Consecration of Man as the sacrament of the community. Sacramental Consultation helps individuals to

find their way to community; the Act of Consecration of
Man strengthens the community of strong individuals.

This connection between the two sacraments that can be
repeated throughout life can be experienced. We spoke
above of the difficulties we can find in concentrating in the
Act of Consecration of Man, if our souls are preoccupied
by undigested thoughts and feelings. The Sacramental
Consultation can help us to prepare for this, by bringing
peace into the turmoil of our souls. The connection goes
deeper still. In the section on the Offering in the Act of
Consecration of Man we described how in this part of the
service, two 'streams' of soul substance flow to the Father:
what issues from the sickness of sin, and what we consciously bring to him as the highest powers of our soul,
thinking, feeling and willing. We can perhaps see the
offering of thoughts in the first line of the verse of the
Sacramental Consultation echoed in the words in the first
part of the Offertory. Perhaps knowing that we have gone
through this movement of offering can make us more aware
of what has 'flowed' to God. When we hear the words in
the Act of Consecration of Man we can for a moment feel
the detritus of our soul leaving us, flowing away.

In the second prayer in the Offertory we turn the highest
forces of our soul to the Father. The conversation with the
priest in the Consultation, the openness to living thinking
and to finding a different source for our will that comes
from hearing the verse: these can be the beginning of the
soul offering. If these two experiences grow in us then we
can experience the Communion as Christ's answer to what
we have brought before the altar. He has taken up the
stream of our soul-substance, both 'bad' and good, into his
own offering, and he gives back to us the transformed
substance, his body and blood.

Marriage

Who takes part?

*Bride and bridegroom; the witnesses and the congregation;
the priest*

BRIDE AND BRIDEGROOM

Marriage is described in the ritual of The Christian Community as 'community of life.' What this means will become clearer in the course of this description. For a beginning we will simply say that in the marriage service a man and a woman come to the altar for the purpose of starting together a 'community of life.' This is one of the turning points of a lifetime, when one way of life ends and another begins. This moment will naturally have been prepared. The preparation consists mainly in making a decision. When the bride and bridegroom stand at the altar, it is the fruit of a decision which they have been preparing for some time before. In the first place the decision that arises out of their discovery that they can love each other is their own personal matter. But once they are sure of their own wishes and begin to think of putting the decision into practice, it is no longer merely a personal matter, but other people begin to be affected and to have a part in it. To put it bluntly, falling in love can be quite a personal affair, but marriage cannot. Its consequences start with the bride and bridegroom and spread to many other people. The decision to marry is threefold in its effects and therefore the preparation should also be threefold.

The first part is spiritual. The love that draws a man and a woman together springs from the urge to make complete what is incomplete. A man is one-sided in one way, a woman in another. Each is a part of the whole human being whose image all of us carry in our thoughts as something we take for granted. Very far back in the history of humanity the division into two halves, into male and female took place.* The longing to unite the two halves into a whole lives since then in human hearts. However, no one is just a man or a woman; each one is a personality and a self, beyond the distinction of sex. The impersonal urge of human nature is interwoven with personal love.

In this sense, marriage is the decision to create something with spiritual reality and power out of forces in the human being that are not naturally in harmony. This is 'community of life'; it is a spiritual reality, uniting what is divided throughout humanity, but uniting it through the individual feeling and willing of the two human hearts. This is where the element of decision is so important. The decision is made by reconciling what is personal and impersonal in two people. It affects their lives, but beyond them, the lives of all other people. If the marriage coming from this decision is successful, healing streams out through the whole community of humanity. From this angle we shall be able to see how the family becomes the fruit of marriage. Children come into the world where the division of the human being into two halves is overcome. They are born out of the human whole and received into the commu-

---

*   Compare *The Sacrament of Marriage,* Kurt von Wistinghausen, Floris 1998

nity of life of father and mother. There was a time when it was said that marriage is there for the sake of the children, but from the point of view described here, we could put it more positively: because there is marriage children can come into the world.

Because marriage is a spiritual event for the bride and bridegroom, for their neighbours and ultimately for the whole of humanity, it is solemnized in a sacrament at the Christian altar. The two other parts to the decision of marriage are not spiritual and therefore in The Christian Community they are not performed in the church. Nevertheless, they should equally have their due.

The first of these belongs to the sphere of social relations and government. Two people, by marrying, alter their legal and social status, therefore their union must be recognized by the government authorities. The registry office provides for this part of marriage and although in some churches it can be performed in the vestry behind the church, this practice is in fact confusing the functions of Church and State.*

The second part belongs to the economic sphere. A marriage brings about a new economic unit, and for this reason there used to be the custom before each wedding of arranging a legal 'marriage settlement,' to cover the property and resources of each party. Nowadays very few people have anything to make a settlement about; nevertheless they have to find an economic basis for their life together and this should be agreed upon beforehand. This is something different from a prenuptial agreement which is concerned not with the economic life of the marriage, but with the division of the assets in the event of a divorce.

---

* The practice in this varies according to the law of the land.

The social and economic parts of the marriage should be
completed first, then the bride and bridegroom come for the
spiritual blessing on their 'community of life.' They have
made a threefold decision that is now becoming the threefold fact of marriage.

THE WITNESSES AND THE CONGREGATION

Two people accompany the bride and bridegroom at the
marriage service and sit one on each side of them. They are
the witnesses. They sit in front of the rest of the congregation and are called publicly by name, but all the
other people present share, in a sense, in their office. They
are all charged by the words of the service to receive
through eyes and ears into their hearts and souls consciousness of the marriage which they are witnessing, and
to give it their continual aid. One may ask at this point:
Can two people not manage their own marriage between
them, do they have to call in other people to help them
from the very beginning? To this one may answer that the
husband and wife need other people to help them, not
because they cannot help each other but because they are
undertaking a task affecting not only themselves but other
people also.

What do those present at a marriage service represent?
Naturally they have come as relatives, neighbours and
friends of the bride and bridegroom to bring their good
wishes and their joy. But once the service begins they all
become something more than this; they become greater
than themselves through what they represent.

A picture will describe this best. If the scene of a
marriage service were painted, not as it appears outwardly,
but as it is inwardly and spiritually, then it would be
portrayed as a circle with the bride and bridegroom in the

centre. One half of the circle would begin with the two
witnesses; it would spread out to include all those who are
present. But it would not stop with the walls of the church:
there would be painted one semicircle after another, full of
human beings, like waves spreading into the world. What
is in the other half of the circle, at the centre of which
bride and bridegroom are standing? It is the divine world,
which looks upon the Sacrament of Marriage as the human
world beholds it. There is another crowd of witnesses,
invisible to our outer eyes, of which our hearts become
aware when we feel that we are taking part in a holy act
performed in the presence of God.

There is a proverb: 'All the world loves a wedding'
which contains a deep truth. The whole world is present at
a wedding, represented by the community of those who
witness it. A wedding has an effect on the whole world
when the marriage creates enduring fruitful community in
the lives of a man and a woman. As marriage is something
which happens not only for the sake of the couple, but for
the world, it is right that the world should help in such a
great undertaking. The witnesses and all present bring
help on behalf of the human world that is waiting for
the achievement of marriage. They help through eyes and
ears, with heart and soul, and they bring their helping will.
They make, as witnesses, a vow never to forget what they
have witnessed, never to lose the helping will they are
sending out to those two friends, whose married life is
beginning.

THE PRIEST

The celebrating priest stands in our imaginary painting in
the centre of the whole circle, with the bride and bridegroom. The first words of the ritual describe his or her

place in the scene. The priest is standing there, acting within it, in the name of Christ. However, the words describe Christ from a particular point of view. He is described as the One who has transformed his working on earth into working in the spirit through his sacrificial deed. The stress is put on the upward direction of what is done by Christ, on transformation. This points to the Resurrection, to all that is begun in that event for the future of the human world. In marriage we encounter what is highest in the human being, selfless love, but we can also face what is most problematic when the marriage goes through difficulties. The priest stands before the bride and bridegroom, before all the witnesses, with the power of the Risen One from whom streams out the creative power for the future of mankind.

What is used?

The vestments used for the marriage service are in the red colour of the Easter season. They express in colour what the priest says in words at the opening of the service: that marriage is celebrated in the sphere of the Resurrection. Red is the colour of triumph. Christ's divine light rises at Easter out of the darkness of death, like the sun rising at dawn. The darkness is overcome by triumphant Light. The Easter mood glows throughout the marriage service, bringing confidence in the future from the promise of strength to overcome, proclaimed by the red colour. Everyone at a wedding may feel grateful for this mood and its promise, for marriage is a part of human life in which the darkness is constantly threatening nearby. It is only too easy for the relations between husband and wife to be darkened and turn destructive. Love and hate are very close to each other in marriage. If love is reversed for some reason it can become hate with a destructive force as great as the creative force of love. So it is right that marriage should begin in the glow of the red which promises the power of the light to overcome the threatening darkness in human nature.

A portrait of Christ is placed on a small table in front of the altar where the bride and bridegroom may see it throughout the ceremony. A head of Christ painted by Leonardo da Vinci is often used. More than other paintings, it shows a face in which neither masculine nor feminine features predominate. It portrays the balance between the two opposite sides of human nature which are represented in a man and a woman. In this face something out of the distant past and distant future of humanity meet. In it there is a memory of very early history — so early that even the Greeks knew of it only as a myth — when the division into the two opposites in the human being had not yet happened. And in it there is the promise of the time to come when, through the Christian forces working in evolution, the split will be healed. The bride and bridegroom see in this picture of Christ's face the truly human quality that their 'community of life' can create if it is fruitful. The split is healed little by little through the creative power of love between a man and a woman. It is widened each time that fruitful love is turned into destroying hate.

The bride and bridegroom each bring a ring to the Sacrament of Marriage. A wise old custom dictates that each should bring the ring of the other to the wedding. Inside each ring the name of the other should be engraved, so that the husband will carry his wife's name within his ring and she will carry his within hers. The ring is the circle within which two halves are made into a whole.

Imagine for a moment how differently a man and a woman think. The woman has, generally speaking, a wider range in her thinking. She catches a new thought quicker, perceives its shades of meaning, takes hold of it with her imagination. She is more ready to seize the picture of the thought, to paint it in colours, to turn it into a vision that rouses a multitude of feelings. But thereby she may more easily become a little fantastic in her thinking. The man is, generally speaking, more logical; he forms the thought more carefully and exactly. He is less quick to carry it over to imagination and feeling, but tends to bring it more into connection with the will. He can better formulate it conceptually, so that other people can get its precise meaning. But masculine thinking easily gets dry, abstract and confined.

A man and a woman thinking harmoniously together can avoid both dangers and make each other's thoughts more fruitful than either could achieve alone. So it is also with the soul life in general. The qualities of a man and a woman can fulfil each other. The woman tends to be more active in feeling and to make every experience one of the heart. The man tends to be more active in the will, and to relate his own will more readily to objective facts. The ring is the sign of the marrying of all the forces in a man and a woman's nature. Furthermore, the ring should be made of gold, the metal belonging in the world outside us to the sun, and within us to our heart. The forces of man and woman are united in heart's love. The rings will continue to be a sign of the love that the two hearts promise to keep towards one another. They signify a partnership of heart and soul beginning at the wedding and going on through life.

On the table with the picture and the rings are laid two short sticks and some red ribbon. During the service the sticks will be tied together in the shape of a cross by the celebrant. For a moment this powerful image of the union of two destinies lights up before the couple who are marrying. There was an old marriage custom by which the bride and bridegroom had to drink together two cups of wine, one sweet and one bitter. The two sticks tied together as a cross strike the same theme. All life with its needs, its cares, its longings, its sickness and pain, as well as its joys and pleasures, is bound together. Husband and wife have each their own destiny; they undertake to share the facts which each brings with his life to the other and to build their community with them. The realities of earthly life speak through the sticks. There are no warnings and admonishments in the words of the service, they are positive and hopeful. Nevertheless, without words, in the sign of the two sticks, a warning note is brought in. The joining of forces denoted in the rings is that part of marriage that makes us long for it. The sharing of earthly facts is the part of marriage that makes people afraid or, when they are married, makes them want to run away from it.

It is here that marriage differs so much from friendship. We tend to be friends with the best qualities of other people; although we would naturally wish to help them in their afflictions and be faithful in the times when their worse qualities are to the fore out of our friendship, nevertheless we are not bound up with their whole nature. Husband and wife, on the other hand, undertake to share all that may happen to each other and still more all the shortcomings, incapacities, unresolved tangles and bodily burdens that each may have. They accept what is destructive along with what is constructive in each other. But there is a note of hope in the sign of the sticks as much as there is of warning. They are bound together in the shape of the cross, to signify the power of the Risen One to transform within human life what is destructive into something fresh and fruitful, to bring life out of death. By this sign the

husband and wife may be reminded that there is a remedy
for the difficulties of married life, lying within their grasp,
which is the magic of transformation.

What is done?

The marriage ritual divides itself naturally into six parts,
which are six stages in a process. When all the people
concerned in the wedding have assembled, the bride and
groom with their two witnesses and the congregation, the
celebrant, standing behind the little table already described,
begins to speak. They speak of the Risen Christ in whose
name they stand before all the people assembled. The first
act of the ritual is to confirm the presence of Christ through
whose working the sacrament will take place.

In The Christian Community this is not understood to
mean that a magical intervention in human affairs is
happening as it were from outside. Christ is understood to
be the bearer of the divine forces within the world of earth.
He is recognized as the Son of God, who was not obliged
by his own nature and destiny to share the earth's life, but
who chose of his freedom to carry the healing power of
God into the sick, fallen world of humanity on the earth.
By his death on the Cross and by his Resurrection, he
united himself with the future of this world and lives in
spirit as an ever-present bringer of healing within it. In this
sense he is at work in the Sacrament of Marriage. The
relation between man and woman has fallen into the
sickness that permeates our world. Of all the spheres of
human life it is one where the most muddle, mistakes and
tragedy are to be found today. Nevertheless, the marriage
service begins by describing the divine Healer, who raises
what begins on earth to fulfilment in the spirit.

In the second act of the ritual, a question is put to both

the bride and groom. On their answer, the further course of the sacrament hinges. Each is asked in turn if he or she wills community of life with the other. The question is put in a very precise way. It speaks of resolves in the world of spirit which accompany us in life. It belongs to the wisdom that comes with old age to see what befalls us in life — good and ill — as the fruit of decisions we made before birth. In the normal course of earthly life we experience these decisions as something that comes to us from outside, as our destiny. It is their destiny that the couple met. However, in view of the emphasis that the Sacrament of Marriage lays on the decision now taken by the couple, it becomes clear that the fact of their decision must be something entirely new, not a consequence of something working from the past. They inscribe this new decision into the realm of spirit to which we normally have no access. This is possible through the fact that they stand face to face with Christ, the bestower and guardian of our true higher self, which makes such decisions.

The affirming 'Yes, I do' that the bride and groom speak is given great weight in the Sacrament of Marriage. It 'seals' their community of life. As far as possible it should be spoken in freedom. Nothing makes us marry — it is a free and sovereign choice, made not *because* of something, but *in order* that we might achieve something together. Such a brief moment requires preparation, and a large part of the preparation for marriage will be concerned with establishing that the decision is indeed free, and helping the couple to understand its implications.

In the third act of the Sacrament of Marriage, the witnesses and all those who are present receive into their consciousness what is said and done and thereby they become something like guardians of the marriage vow, as was described earlier. It may be important for them later to remind the couple of the moment of their decision and of the freedom which was the basis for it.

In the fourth act of the ritual the celebrant gives the rings to bridegroom and bride. This is followed by the binding of the two sticks with red ribbon, after which they are held aloft as the symbol of union. The joining together of a man and a woman into community of life has been expressed and sealed in words; now it is incarnated, as it were, a stage further through the sign of rings and sticks. This solemn act implies a union that will last.

People may well feel anxious about the responsibility implied by this service. In these times of change and uncertainty many of us may ask: can I actually tie myself to another person for life? Can I make any promise and be certain that I shall be able to keep it for years to come? Such anxious questions bring up the whole problem of divorce and re-marriage. The Christian Community is a Church without dogma. It is a Church for people who think for themselves. Consequently there are no rules about divorce. Human destinies are very complex; one situation is never quite like another. But wherever and whenever such problems arise it is good to return to the words of the marriage service. They provide a standard for judgment that would hinder anyone from taking marriage lightly. Those who take up community of life in the sense of those words, do so intending that it shall last. They may need to renew the intention from time to time; they might even fail to keep it, but they will receive the marriage sacrament in the will that their community shall endure. If they take seriously the importance of their decision with its far-reaching dimensions, they will see that on one level at least what is inaugurated in marriage cannot be dissolved, as it has been inscribed in the world of spirit.

The fifth act consists of an address given by the cele-

brant in his or her own words. It should help the couple
and the community to grasp the importance of what happens in the Sacrament of Marriage, and it should relate this
in some way to the personal situation of the couple.

The sixth act is a blessing. It is given first in words, in
the name of the Trinity, for the help of those who are being
married and through them for the whole of humanity. It is
then given in a gesture, confirmed by an 'Amen,' that
brings the ritual to an end. Nowadays it is not easy to be
sure what a blessing means and does. Unlike the people of
whom we read in the Old Testament, we do not expect
very much to happen if someone says 'bless you' or even
if he says 'curse you.' However, this is our loss. It is important to discover anew that a true act of blessing bestows
a grace upon those who receive it, a grace greater than that
which they bear within themselves. The act of blessing
adds strength and power to the marriage, illuminating it
with a warm, bright light of spirit. that will not fade from
the hearts of husband and wife, if they are careful to keep
it in sight.

What happens?

Each time the Sacrament of Marriage is celebrated, it
creates a new fact in the world. It creates this fact in the
destinies of the two people who are married and in those of
all the people connected with them. It creates the fact in
society as a whole, in which a new family, that is to say a
new social unit, appears. It creates the fact again for 'all
mankind,' in that the original split into male and female in
the nature of the human being begins to be healed.

The sacrament is an act of creation which we can
imagine by comparing it with the building of a house. First
the plan of a house exists as an idea in the minds of the

architect and the builder. Then the process of building begins, the house becomes visible and tangible; the idea becomes a physical fact and the house is built. So it is with marriage.

It begins with the idea of the community of life between a man and a woman. Two separate people begin to share this idea. They find it in the spiritual sphere, where human souls cherish their highest purposes of life. Their spirit-born resolve is present in their hearts and minds before the marriage service begins. During its celebration the idea and the resolve become incarnated into an earthly fact. They are incarnated first of all in the word spoken by the bride and bridegroom and received into the consciousness of all those present. They are incarnated still further in the physical symbols of the rings and the sticks. The whole is an act of creation, whereby an idea becomes an earthly fact.

Thinking along these lines one should not overlook the point that the marriage service is intended to originate new facts but not to bring them to a conclusion. Marriage starts from the sacrament but it will go on being created year by year. It is one of those facts that never 'are,' but are always 'becoming.' Marriages can come to grief just because husbands and wives begin to take them for granted, or for any other reasons cease to go on creating them. The sacrament brings ideas into facts so that they may begin and continue to live and be created in the world of earth.

At the end of the service the new fact of the marriage is blessed in the name of the Trinity. Marriages that are not celebrated through the sacrament are also facts of the earthly world. However, they have not been originated by calling on the presence of Christ, that he may unite them with his guidance of world history. The image of the building of a house which has already been used as an illustration, may be used again in a transformed sense.

Christ is the builder of the heavenly City, the New Jerusalem, described at the close of the Revelation to St John as
the vision of humanity redeemed and re-created. He builds
the Holy City with every fact of human life that can be
transformed by him, that can be Christianized. When a
marriage is created in his Name, it is a fact that can be
built into the City.

The Anointing

Who takes part?

The one who is dying; the friends; the priest

THE ONE WHO IS DYING

The services of The Christian Community can accompany someone throughout the whole process of preparing for death and dying. If it is possible, a Sacramental Consultation can be held as the beginning. This will ideally be the culmination of a series of conversations reviewing the life which is approaching its end. This is followed by the Communion which can be brought to the sick bed. Just before the death takes place the sacrament of the Anointing is celebrated. Three days after death the Funeral Service may be held. On the Saturday following the funeral, or on a Saturday soon afterwards, the Memorial Act of Consecration of Man may take place. These services accompany the soul of the one who dies all the way through the gate of death into the life beyond, through words and deeds and by the prayers of the friends who take part.

Death and birth are the most dramatic events of earthly life. In death the soul returns to the world of spirit from which it came at birth. There is always something akin to death in birth and to birth in death. The beings who dwell in the world of spirit saw the soul die away from them into birth; in death they receive again their companion at the end of the journey along the ways of earth. Among the old saints of the Celtic Church the death day was always called the 'birthday' and often, as one of them was dying, their friends could perceive a joyful host of angels coming to meet the departing soul. For our feeling today dying has become more of a passing into the unknown than it was for theirs. But if we observe the mood and behaviour of those whom we meet as they are nearing death we shall be able to feel in them the first gleam of the new life they are approaching. It is true that some feel crushed in the face of death and the ending of their life. However, others look back and see what has been missing in their life and resolve on a new beginning that shall make good the past. These are the ones through whom the true mood of death is speaking. To live over again and to live better is the wish quickened in the soul by the nearness of death, and this is a hint of the new life beginning beyond the gate.

But, though there is the touch of birth in dying, there is also the pain of parting. The departing souls have to leave the earthly presence of friends and dear ones, they have to leave interests and achievements on earth, their finished destinies and, greatest of all wrenches, they have to leave the house of the body. To part from the body is like a turning inside out of one's whole being. It is naturally a cause for fear, to face the complete changing of consciousness that goes with this. Ultimately the fear of death — whatever form it takes in different people — is really one and the same fear, that of losing one's self. And together with this fear goes the sense of loneliness. Friends may bring comfort and help, but in the last resort the dying soul faces the universe alone. Fear and loneliness are the inevitable pains of death. But it would be a hasty assumption to believe that its pains are only negative. They prick the soul awake — more awake than ever in life before — that it shall be alert to perceive the world that is opening out beyond the gate. Pain accompanies all the great events in human life, from birth with its pangs and its labour onwards till death. It is the sign that something great is happening, that the soul is exchanging one existence for another. This should not imply an unsympathetic attitude towards those who are suffering in the struggle to die. They need every comfort and relief, but they will find it most truly from those friends who have insight into the meaning of their pain.

Thus it is both a beginning and an ending when a human soul approaches death. In this situation the sacraments which the soul has known in life can be a great help: together with a priest, a human being can look over his or her life, seeing it now from this clearest of vantage points, before the threshold of death. This review and a gaze ahead at the trials to come can be the content of a final Sacramental Consultation. Then, for the last time on the earth, the soul is prepared to receive the Communion. And finally the Sacrament of Anointing may be brought as the last holy act of this life and the promise of the new life to begin after death.

THE FRIENDS

The words of the Anointing are addressed to the one who is dying and the service is held at the bedside. But as many friends as are able to come or as many as the one who is sick can bear in the room at once may be present. More than almost any other experience does this one bind, in the last hours of life, the hearts of the friends who are left on earth to the heart of the one who is going on before them. The old friendship on earth can be transformed in these moments into the new friendship which can outlast death.

At the Funeral Service and the memorial service the friends are again present with many more, some of whom may be less closely connected. There they will lift their thoughts to the soul of the friend who is already on the other side of death. The thoughts spoken in the service will help them to accompany in heart and mind the first steps of the friend on the way beyond the gate.

It is commonly felt to be a special duty to attend the funeral of someone to whom one is linked by relationship, work or friendship. It is at the least a token of respect for the one who has died and for the lifetime which is now closed. It is much more than this for those whose hearts are full of sorrow at losing the presence among them of a loved and trusted friend. For them it is a solemn, sad farewell. But in whatever mood the friends attend a funeral or an Anointing they should be able to realize that they share their feelings with the friend who is passing through death. If their own sorrow is too absorbing, they may be unable to give to their loved one what he or she needs from them as strengthening. The friends can help greatly if they are able to put aside the sense of their own loss and think with gratitude of their friend's life, of its achievements and trials and of all that it has meant to those who have shared in it. At every funeral there should be as much gratitude as regret in the hearts of those present if they would give their departing friend the warmth he or she needs. It is important that they should be present as much for the sake of accompanying their friend's soul in thought, as for the sake of their own leave-taking.

The Anointing and the Funeral Service may become for the friends as well as for the one who dies, as much a new beginning as a farewell. Those who are beyond the gate of death are not lost for those who are alive on the earth. But the consciousness of them may be lost if those who are left behind do not strive to find a new form of relationship with them. We do not see the dead with our earthly eyes nor do we hear them with our earthly ears. Nevertheless, it is possible to hold conversations with them, to accompany them in the experiences of their new life, to share with them some of the problems of our life on earth. This may be done not by outer, but by inner activity. Another kind of thought, another kind of listening, speaking and meeting from those of ordinary life are needed. But these can be found and cultivated by all those who wish to have fellowship with their friends who have died. The starting-point is to find a meeting-place in common; it will be found in thoughts which are as real and true in the worlds of spirit, where the souls dwell after death, as in the world of earth. The Anointing, the Funeral Service and the Memorial Act of Consecration of Man offer such thoughts to help us to found this fellowship in the moment of death itself.

THE PRIEST

When someone is in danger of death, it is a matter of course to send for a doctor. But nowadays it is not nearly so much a matter of course to send for the priest to come and celebrate the sacrament for the dying. It is even felt by some people to be equivalent to a death sentence or to giving up all hope of life to ask the priest to come. But this is a misunderstanding. There is no harm in someone receiving the Anointing and then recovering again. In fact this sacrament may in itself bring about a crisis and cause the patient to turn back again to life on the earth. Should this not happen, should the process of dying set in and death take place, then the sacrament can make the passing of the soul more calm and confident. It is one of the cruelties common today to leave the one who is dying alone when the doctor can do no more and to omit to request a priest to do his or her work too, by which the struggle of death may be soothed and hallowed.

In celebrating the services for the dying and the dead, the priest stands on the threshold between the world of earth which the soul of the dying friend is leaving and the world of spirit which it is entering. The words of the ritual which the priest speaks sound forth to those who have gathered together as earthly friends, but they sound forth as much to the beings of the spirit world who come to receive the departing soul in their midst. The words go with the soul of the one who is dying from the earth into the world on the other side of the gate until in the prayer spoken at the conclusion of the Memorial Service he or she is released into the boundless, deathless worlds of God.

What is used?

For the Anointing vestments of the colour of the season are used, while for the Funeral Service and the Memorial Service black vestments over white are used. This may appear at first to stress the dark, sad side to death and to omit the hope that equally belongs to it. But we have to bear in mind that it is our earthly eyes that see the black, and this truly expresses the dark, earthly side of death. It is different for those who have died; they see at a funeral nothing of the gloomy colour, but only the bright reflection that shines from the black in the world beyond the senses. Those who are present in the body and have the impression of the black colour can find consolation in the words of the services. They are not dark in mood, but express the light that shines from beyond the gate of death.

In the Anointing oil is used. In the foregoing description of the Sacrament of Baptism, we described how a child is christened with water, salt and ash. These are the substances whose forces work to lead the soul into the material world of earth. The oil is the corresponding substance whose forces bear the soul up into the living world of spirit. The oil is taken from the fruit of the olive tree. It is formed when what the tree sends up from its roots to the flower combines with what the air, light and warmth of the heavens shed down from above. We can learn much about the essential nature of a substance by studying where it is formed. Olive oil does not come from the surface of the earth but is produced a little way above it on the branches of the tree. Its origin is midway between earth and heaven. This makes it by nature a kind of intermediary; this it is also in its effect when taken from the tree for human use. Plants express in substance what in the human world would be a quality of soul. The oil embodies as a natural force what, humanly speaking, would be devotion and love to the spirit. The longing to strive towards the world of spirit, to be united with it once more, is the whole of its nature. Through this it can act as a kind of helper to the departing soul on the passage to the world of spirit. It unites with the soul's own love of the spirit to help it come free from the body and pass on into the sphere of soul existence.

In the Funeral service two other substances are united in their working with the words that are spoken. The coffin containing the body is sprinkled with consecrated water and censed with the smoke of incense. Both these substances express the metamorphosis from one state to another. Water has the power to dissolve matter and change it into a state where something new can evolve. Incense has the power of transforming itself from a hard gum into heavenward streaming smoke and scent, so thoroughly that nothing of its substance remains. Water and incense are helpers in the change of nature that comes with death. Water helps the soul's last parting from the body that is dissolving away into the existence of the earth. Incense lifts it up and gives it wings to rise heavenward; as the oil is the soul's first assistant on its passage from the earth, so water and incense are its last.

What is done?

'He died as he lived' is a saying sometimes used to describe a manner of dying. In actual fact experience shows that this could be said over most death beds. Death is the culmination of a lifetime, and all that has gone before in living prepares the manner in which the soul meets death. Great changes may often take place in the last stages of life, not only in those who die of illness but also in those whose passing is brought on by violence and accident. But those who have seen deeper into the hearts of the people in whom great changes appear at death, recognize that the changes unveil a deeper part in them that was always there, but could only break through at the extremity.

Hidden sides of character and personality may well appear plainly in death, for its nearness breaks a spell that has been active for the greater part of life. We all of us carry a being about with us who is a kind of parasite in the soul, and who, if we are not constantly on the watch, introduces many of his actions and reactions into our behaviour. It confuses many a character and clouds much greatness of soul. It could be described as the 'personal devil' of each one of us. In death it makes its escape and leaves the true person revealed. Change of this kind is a part of every deathbed, and it makes no contradiction to the fact that ultimately people die as they have lived.

This being so, what can be done at death in The Christian Community depends somewhat on how far the dying one has lived previously with its services and ways of thinking. It is possible to hold the Funeral Service by itself when this is requested for someone whose connection was a distant one. But those who are nearer to The Christian Community will realize what it signifies that the whole process of dying can be hallowed and that the Funeral Service is only a portion of the whole. They will ask a priest to come to them before the last extremity. If this is done in good time, the Anointing can be prepared fully in the way described above. Why this should be so follows naturally from the description of death, which has already been given. It can be recalled by the motto of a famous dying Queen: 'My end is my beginning.'

To make a good end to life one should look back while one still has the consciousness to do so, gather together the threads, and try to perceive the pattern as a whole, helped by the insight that the nearness of death can give. This will in itself help to make a good beginning in the afterlife when the soul will have to work back through past experiences again. Such a review of life is blessed at its conclusion with the words of the Sacramental Consultation, as it was described in a foregoing chapter. It is then sealed by the giving of the Communion, the consecrated bread and wine, which are the medicine for the sickness of sin.

When this is completed, either on the same occasion or at a later one, the Anointing is celebrated. The Service begins with a reading from the seventeenth chapter of the Gospel of St John. These words are the prayer to the Father-God spoken before his death on the Cross by Christ for all human souls who find their way to him. Not for humanity as a whole does the Son pray at this moment to the Father, but for the individual souls as he knows them, so to speak, by name. Through these words, the dying soul may become aware that what we call on earth 'death' is called by Christ in the Gospels 'going to the Father.' The soul may feel itself in the hands of Christ, carried in his keeping over the threshold into the realms of the Father.

After the reading, three crosses are made with oil, one over each eye, and one in the centre of the forehead. All the other words of the ritual are spoken as the signs are made. They speak of Christ as the Guide and Helper of the soul on the way through death. What is brought about in this sacrament is done equally in words and in signs. The signs are deeds that change events. The event of dying is transformed under the three signs of the cross. The cross is in itself a sign, in which ending becomes beginning and death becomes life. Christ met death on the Cross, but he was the stronger. He overcame death and transformed the cross into the sign of life. Since then each human being bears the cross within him, as the promise of what Man shall become. When we stand with our head held up to the heavens, our arms stretched into the widths of space, our feet planted on the earth and know ourselves in this shape, related to heights, widths and depths, then we become aware of the creating power of the cross within. Therefore, it has become the sign of life. As the sign of death becoming life, it is made in the sacrament of the Anointing.

The Anointing should be celebrated while life is still present in the body. It is advisable that it should be held while the dying person is still conscious although this is not a condition. Three days after death the Funeral Service should be held. It is inadvisable to do so before the three days are over, because the soul lingers near the body for that length of time. The three days can become a festival in themselves, when the friends understand how to arrange them. Unfortunately, it is often necessary to send the body to a mortuary or undertaker's chapel, but if this can be avoided, the dead person can be kept in his or her own room and laid out in the familiar space. The room will be filled with the holy atmosphere of death, the friends will come there to sit quietly, to pray and to read to their dead friend who will receive comfort from their presence, and they will receive calm and uplifting of thought and feeling from the one who has died.

What is important above all in this time is that the one who has died should experience peace. The body should be moved as little as possible; any noise or disruption should be kept to a minimum. It is not necessary to maintain a 'wake' around the clock. The three-day leave-taking may be a holy, quiet time for all concerned. In countries with a hot climate, the dissolution is naturally quicker and the time of pause is inevitably shorter. But in countries of moderate climate the three days should elapse before the body is buried or burned. After three days it will become clear at a glance that the soul has finished with the body and has let it go. Then is the moment for the funeral.

The Funeral Service in The Christian Community is in two parts. The first part should, if circumstances permit, be held in the room in which the lying in has taken place. The friends who have helped to make a festival of the three days will be accustomed to look at the dead face of their friend, finding it something not to be afraid of but to admire. During the short service they will look on it for the last time and afterwards the coffin will be closed. The second part of the Funeral Service is held either at the side of the grave or in the crematorium. The Funeral Services are addressed almost entirely to the one who has died and to God; they do not offer comfort to those who have been left behind, but ask of them that they accompany the departed soul in thought and prayer. It is perhaps a deeper comfort to give a spiritual task than to offer kind words. It is well known that, in times of shock, it is important to help people to mobilize their own resources and to feel that there is something which they themselves can do. At the end of the second part, the body is either sunk into the earth or passed over into the furnace of the crematorium.

The second part of the Funeral Service contains an address, usually given by the priest, concerning the destiny, work and personality of the dead friend. Such an address serves to awaken memories and understanding in the minds of those who have come to the funeral. But it is of service also to the soul of the one who has died. If we bear in mind that the first great task of the soul in the life after death is to understand the earthly life it has just concluded, and, with the help of spiritual beings, to work on it to transform it, we can see the funeral address as a kind of 'visiting card' that is sent with the soul into the spiritual world.

The Funeral is followed on a Saturday morning soon after it by the Memorial Service. Each day of the week has its own character; Saturday is the one that brings the souls of the departed nearest to what is being done on earth. On a Saturday therefore the Act of Consecration of Man may be celebrated in special memory of someone who has died. At all seasons, the vestments are black on such occasions and the Gospel reading is taken from the story of the Resurrection in St Mark's Gospel. At the close of the service, after the Communion, a prayer is inserted in which the departed friend is prayed for by name. The prayer speaks of the soul's new life in the realms of the God the Father. With this last act the departed soul is accompanied by the prayers of friends on earth right into the life after death. From then on they may include their dead friend among 'those who have died,' of whom it is said in each Act of Consecration of Man that they join in bringing the Offering. And they may ask his or her help in the later prayer, which speaks of the 'sheltering power' that the departed friends can send to those who are still engaged in the struggle of life on earth.

What happens?

'My end is my beginning.' This saying from the hour of death, which is quoted now a second time, sounds like a riddle. And rightly so, for it puts into words the riddle, which perplexes every heart that asks itself: What happens at death? Nevertheless, the saying itself hints at the direction where an answer can be found, through the possessive pronoun 'my.' Death is something that belongs to myself, for which I can use the word 'my,' if I have insight enough to recognize my own part in it. From one aspect, death seems to come upon me from outside and it is a necessary part of experience that this should be so. The tragedy of suicide is that it overlooks this fact. But there is another, more secret aspect, that does not contradict the first, though it sounds like a paradox to say so. Death is an event brought upon me by myself. It comes about always through an intimate decision made in the depths of my being, so deep that it rarely comes to ordinary consciousness. It is certainly not my self as I know it every day, and which plans my affairs, that makes the decision. That would be the same as suicide. But it is my higher self that has its existence in world-heights and speaks to me in the depths of the soul, who makes the decision. This self can act with divine wisdom and its actions in my life appear to my ordinary self to be events coming from outside. They may be events that seem to this other self to be hindrances or tragedies. Our consciousness of the higher self is so dim, that the two selves are not always of the same mind. It is in this sense death is my own decision.

When the decision is once made, it takes varying lengths of time to carry it out. For some people it is a matter of weeks before the soul actually leaves the body. For others it may be a matter of minutes, seconds, or, from an earthly standpoint, of no time at all. But everyone goes through the same process in dying; the difference is in the time it takes and in the apparent cause, whether natural or violent. The higher self makes the decision to call the soul back from the earth, the soul has to recognize the call and the body has to release the soul. When the last breath is drawn, the soul is breathed out and passes over into the world of the spirit. Then the garment of life that has clothed the body dissolves more slowly into the universe and the physical substance of the body disintegrates into the substance of the earth. Then the process of dying is finished.

Through the Anointing and services of death Christ enters into this process. He accompanies the soul along the way to the gate of death and out beyond it to the world of the Father-God. The Anointing is the sacrament that holds in it the decision to leave the earth. The decision may be made before it is celebrated, afterwards, or within the service itself. And it may happen, as has already been described, that the decision is reversed through the sacrament and a departing soul turns back again earthward. Sometimes the actual moment of the decision stands out clearly, at others it is kept hidden.

All this may vary but the Anointing always expresses and assists the decision, passing it into the hands of Christ that his peace may overcome fear and loneliness. His presence lightens up for the soul the working of its own higher self so that the knowledge of lasting existence and divinely guided destiny may stream in. The soul will be able to feel, if it opens trustfully to accept the sacrament, like a traveller along a dark, uncertain road who finds all at once that he is accompanied by someone who goes in front and lights up the way. And not only does this Companion know the road, and can show where it is leading but he gives warmth and courage to the heart on the way. The peace that can come over someone who is dying and has passed beyond the fear of death is the gift of this Companion whose presence is sought in the Anointing. Knowing about the decision, taken at the deepest level of a human soul, can help the family and friends in their prayers for the one who is dying. Natural though it is to wish it, a little reflection will show that it cannot be right simply to pray that the other one might not die. After all we have to accept our mortality and indeed try to see wisdom in it. What will be important rather is to pray that the one who is ill should be able to make the right decision — that, particularly if great pain, drugs or technical intervention are clouding their consciousness, they may hear the voice of the higher self and have the courage to take the next step.

The Funeral and Memorial Services are held after the decision has been carried out. They reveal Christ leading the soul beyond the gate of death into the worlds of spirit. He leads from one world to the other. It is he especially, in whose presence the souls who have remained on this side of the gate can meet with those who have passed through it. He stands on the threshold of death; in him the purpose of earth existence is revealed. The dying see this revelation as they pass on, but they look back to their friends on earth, seeing in them those through whom the work of Christ may be done. They experience themselves as the seers and ourselves as the doers. They expect from us that we will fulfil Christ's deeds on earth. Every thought of our departed friends should awaken us afresh to the responsibility for doing, which is our part as long as we live on earth.

The foregoing description of dying relates to the experiences of adults, but it will not hold good for children. They have come so short a way through the gate of birth, that they can easily slip back to the world they scarcely have left. They are also called back by a divine decision, but they can go without the same wrench, the same fearful turning inside out of themselves. Therefore The Christian Community has a different Funeral Service for children under fourteen years of age. It is directed to comforting the parents and friends who are left behind. It describes for them the return to the worlds of God of the soul they had received for its short stay on earth. The very different character it has from the service described before shows how truly these services meet the facts of human life. All of them have the purpose of bringing into the darkness of death the light of Christ. He is the One who leads human souls into death, so that they find on the far side of the gate the birth into the life of the spirit.

The Ordination of Priests

Who takes part?

The one who is consecrated; the community of priests; the congregation

THE ONE WHO IS CONSECRATED

The Ordination of Priests is celebrated for the sake of all the other sacraments. It is given to those men and women who undertake to become celebrants of the sacraments and preachers of the Gospel. It is essential to the nature of the sacraments that they are spiritual-physical acts beyond human power to perform. No one out of their individual will or capacities could bring them about. Everyone who is called to become a celebrant must be placed in a stream of spiritual grace. The Sacrament of Ordination is the means by which a candidate for the priesthood can be endowed with this grace of God. Upon receiving it, they make a vow to undertake the holy task of celebrating the sacraments for the rest of their life. The vow is the answer to the spiritual gift of the power to celebrate. Such a grace is not a personal gift; it is given for the sake of the sacraments and of all those who wish to take part in them. Once given, it brings the obligation to use it in the service of Christianity and to continue so doing until death itself ends the task. Just because a power beyond the ordinary is given by Ordination, so it requires obligations beyond the ordinary.

Even from this one fact it is clear what an important moment this is in the life of the one who is consecrated. No kind of work is more binding, none affects the life and destiny of those who undertake it more deeply. Without exaggeration it can be said that Ordination is the most decisive turning point in a lifetime. It does not mean taking up a new job so much as taking up a new life. One may wonder: How can anyone face so binding a decision for so long in these days of uncertainty, when no one can see what the next year will bring, and few people can be sure of their own ability to make up their minds about any important matter. But it can be done when the decision comes out of the spirit, from God. The usual pros and cons about starting new work — whether it will be well paid and lead to promotion, whether it will make one happy, or satisfy one's family, about whether one has the talents and aptitude for it, are of no use in deciding whether or not to enter the priesthood. Such considerations can only hinder the decision. The Christian Community is as much a pioneer movement as the early Christian Church. Its worldly advantages are small. But it offers an opportunity of a kind most rare in our present time, that is to say, the opportunity to devote oneself with every energy to work which can only begin out of a high spiritual decision. It is the opportunity to dedicate one's self and one's life to the progress of Christianity.

The decision, to be complete, must come from three different directions. It must be matured in the candidate's own heart. Candidates will need to find, by a process that may be a long one, whether their wish to become a priest proceeds from their higher self that guides their life on earth from the world of spirit. They will seek to discover whether this purpose is one of the lasting purposes that are bound up with the spiritual core of their being. Only if the wish reveals itself as a spiritual purpose will they have the strength to remain faithful to it. The decision has also to mature in the hearts and minds of those who are already priests of The Christian Community. Their part of the decision is made in common, but if they are unable to agree, there are holders of offices within the whole movement, whose duty it is to decide. However, the decision is not only a human one, it is also divine. The intention to seek Ordination needs to be offered as a question to the divine world and it is necessary to look for and listen for the answer. It may come in the form of outer events that confirm or deny it, or in the form of an inner conviction. But 'come it will' and in no other way can such a decision ever be established as the will not of Man but of God.

Ordination is preceded by preparation for the work of the priest. This is not so much a matter of learning, as of becoming a priest in one's whole character. What is learned is not properly learnt for the work until it has been digested and transformed into 'second nature.' Indeed, training for the priesthood could be described as growing a priestly nature as 'second nature.' In this sense the priest's education will last for the rest of the priest's life, but the beginning should be made in the time of preparation. There is a seminary in Stuttgart, Germany, which offers seven half-year semesters of instruction in theological disciplines and a broad range of other subjects. In line with the conception of priesthood in The Christian Community, the training is not narrowly focused or academic. It is a training of the whole human being which includes regular artistic activity, movement, speech training, as well as the challenges of a communal lifestyle. There are no formal examinations, the setting being small enough that assessment can be undertaken individually. Additionally, there are orientation courses for the priesthood in various countries.

A word should be added about one departure from the old customs of the Churches, in the priesthood of The Christian Community. Both women and men are ordained without distinction. Times change and human beings change with them. The way in which men and women differ from each other is no longer the same in this century as it was in earlier ones. Even if there was a time when it was justified to restrict the priesthood to men, this is no longer the case. From the foundation of The Christian Community onwards, women have shared as priests in all its work.

THE COMMUNITY OF PRIESTS

Those who receive ordination in The Christian Community enter into a new spiritual relationship to two circles or communities of people. The one is the congregation, towards whom they are to be 'shepherds of souls,' as the Ordination states. The other is the existing circle of priests, of which they now become members. This double relationship is expressed in the fact that the Ordination ceremonies are in two parts, the one being held in private among the priests, the other in public before the congregation. It is expressed in the Sacrament of Ordination itself in an act that takes place about halfway through. The celebrant walks, holding the cup which contains the consecrated elements, around all the priests who are present, enclosing them and the those who have just been ordained within a circle. All those who share in common the responsibility for the new Christian sacraments and the promise of their lives to their service are enclosed in a circle. It would be a mistake to suppose that the circle is there in order to keep other people out, or to imply that those within the circle are better people than those without. It should not be forgotten

that priests are ordained because they are aware that they
are not able to celebrate the sacraments without the grace
of God. An act of humility is implied at the outset. The
circle is there, not to exclude, but to concentrate. It draws
together those who have a task to share too big for any one
of them alone.

It is hard for us in our present stage of development
truly to co-operate with each other. We have reached a
stage in our development where it is right that we are in-
dividualists. It is natural for us to feel that we must protect
ourselves against our neighbours, shutting the portcullis of
our castle against them. Christianity, however, embodies a
truth which goes beyond the principle of individualism. We
may remember once more Christ's words: 'For where two
or three are gathered in my name, there am I in the midst
of them,' (Matt.18:20). This saying does not deny the
personal, but it calls us to become larger-minded, to grow
on to a new stage, where individuals unite in community.
Creating such Christian community represents a great
challenge. But experience shows that we can best meet this
challenge when all the single minds are directed towards a
common spiritual aim. The circle of priests is such a
community of individuals striving constantly to find each
other in their common task and to work with each other in
common service. In this sense, for the sake of the common
task, they are bound together in a circle.

The erzoberlenker,* or leader of The Christian Community, performs Ordinations wherever possible. He does so
on behalf of the whole priesthood. But this does not signify
that no other may do so in principle. In The Christian
Community all priests are ordained for the celebration of
all sacraments. The different offices in the Church do not

---

* The name has been retained from the German title.

imply different degrees of ordination. The offices are positions of administrative responsibility. There is one consecration to the priesthood for all.

THE CONGREGATION

The Congregation, the second of the two circles of people previously described, gathers at the public service of Ordination. In the renewed sacramental life of The Christian Community, the congregation does not simply watch what takes place in the Ordination and receive the priests on the authority of the Church. The congregation has a dual role in the Sacrament of Ordination. On the one hand it is called upon to pray with the celebrant and the circle of priests that the candidates may be worthy and the Ordination take place rightly. On the other hand they are called upon to recognize what has happened, and recognize those who have been ordained as 'shepherds of souls.' Only then will they be able to fulfil their tasks as priests. Once again, as in the Act of Consecration of Man, the stream of grace which flows in from the divine world meets the efforts of human beings and helps them to become spiritually effective.

What is used?

The public service of Ordination is held within the Act of Consecration of Man. In each of the four parts of this service which have already been described, prayers and ceremonies are added by which the one who is being consecrated receives step by step the signs and substance of priesthood.

This is expressed in the first place through the vestments. At the opening of the service, the candidate enters

wearing only the black cassock covered by the white alb.
We have discussed the significance of these vestments
above (see p. 41). In summary, we might say that these two
are, as their colours show, the tokens of life and death in
the human being.

In the course of the Ordination, the one who is being
consecrated is vested with the stole as the symbol of
priesthood. When the stole is worn it takes on the form of
a yoke; it can be seen as representing the Christian task
which the priest takes on. It inscribes the sign of the cross
on the breast of the priest. On receiving this, the priest
reads the Gospel from the altar for the first time. The book
of the Gospels and the book in which the words of the
ritual are written down are both tokens that the words
spoken do not proceed from the personal mind of the
speaker, but are divine words spoken with a human voice.
Behind this token, there can be seen as the pattern of the
Christian priesthood the figure of John the Baptist. In the
Prologue of St John's Gospel, we hear of the creation of
the world by the Word of God. Into this cosmic drama,
John the Baptist appears, the first human being mentioned
in the Gospel of St John. He is asked who he is and
answers: 'I am the voice ...' The priest is the human voice
through whom the Word of God speaks. This is expressed
in the symbols of the stole and the book.

Later on in the course of the Ordination rites, the one
who is being consecrated is invested with the chasuble.
This is the vestment whose colour changes with the seasons
of the year, worn only in the Act of Consecration of Man,
the service in which the Transubstantiation takes place. It
is the symbol of the power to consecrate the elements of
bread and wine. Here too, the picture of John the Baptist
can shed light on this symbol. After his death at the hands
of Herod, John's martyrdom bore fruit for the other

disciples. He became after his death the guardian spirit of the Twelve who walked with Jesus Christ. The Gospels describe their first act after his death as that of assisting their Master at the Feeding of the Five Thousand. What is this act but the first deed of Christ towards instituting the Christian Sacrament? From this time on the disciples are getting ready to receive the chasuble, to become the first celebrants of the Christian Sacrament. The spirit of John accompanies them, guarding for them in spirit the symbol of the chasuble that is waiting to descend upon them to seal their priesthood.

As soon after the Ordination service as possible, the new priests celebrate the Act of Consecration of Man for the first time. Before they begin they receive the final element of their vestments, the biretta. This is the three-pointed black hat which is the sign of office within the Community, worn whenever the priest enters the room to celebrate a ritual or sacrament, and also when the priest in vestments speaks with their own words, for instance in sermons. The newly-ordained priest puts the biretta on for the first time in the presence of the congregation, as the prelude to the first celebration.

The substance used in the Ordination rites is oil. We have spoken about the spiritual nature of this substance in the description of the Anointing, the sacrament for the dying. In what can be experienced in the Ordination itself, there is an element connected with death. Within the soul of the one who is consecrated, a new, priestly nature has to be born. Within the human soul of the priest, a 'priestly soul,' something more than personal, should be born. Such a birth as this cannot happen without the personality accepting the death of much in itself. In soul the new priests will feel being born again out of an inner sacrifice, out of an inner death. But those who are willing to lose their souls

will find that they save, not the same soul, but the new soul
of the priest. Being consecrated, they die and are born
again.

From time immemorial oil has been used to anoint kings
and priests. Indeed, the word 'Christ' is the Greek word
used in the Gospels for the Hebrew 'Messiah,' which
simply means 'anointed one.' The kings and priests of the
ancient Jewish people were 'Messiahs.' An ancient wisdom
about earthly substances recognized in the holy oil the
power to make the earthly transparent for the working of
the spirit: thus it was used for those whose task it was to
be open for the working into earthly life a particular spiritual being. Priests in The Christian Community are anointed
with the oil of death, that the living grace of the spirit may
pour into them.

What is done?

At the Ordination service the Act of Consecration of Man
is celebrated as it always is, with two omissions. The creed
is not read, and there is no general communion. The
prayers for the consecration of priests are woven into its
four parts and those who are receiving the consecration
stand with the celebrant at the altar. It is as if they would
follow him into the act of celebration step by step as the
ritual proceeds. All other priests who are present sit in their
vestments on either side of the altar and behind the candidates, making visible through their position the community
of the priesthood into which the new priests are being taken
up. The congregation sits facing the altar as on other occasions, and forms the community of Christians whose spirit
is acknowledging the Ordination. Two servers represent the
congregation at the altar; one gives the responses that put
this acknowledgement into words. In this sacrament we can

experience again something about which we have spoken earlier in our descriptions of the other sacraments. To be present at a priest's Ordination is to share in the most important event in their destiny and to change in a subtle but lasting way one's relation to them, just as one establishes a relationship to another life by being present at a Baptism or by witnessing a Marriage. It may be that these relationships born of the sacraments never become personal connections but in the weaving of wider destinies, and in the history of The Christian Community, they form living, creative ties between human souls.

At the beginning of the Gospel reading, the first of the four parts in the Act of Consecration of Man, the prayers of Ordination begin. One priest may be consecrated alone or several together. In the first prayer they are all offered to God, the Eternal Ground of the World, to serve, cherish and work for his wisdom and working in the world. There is also a solemn appeal to God the Father that he may prevent the Ordination from continuing, if the candidates are unworthy. Then the prayers of the Gospel reading continue, and after them comes the first act of Ordination addressed to those who are being consecrated. They are charged to serve Christ and, following this, they receive the priestly dignity in the sign of the stole, hearing as they receive it the words which describe the priest's task. Thereupon the candidates read the opening words of St John's Gospel as their first act at the altar. In this manner the nature of priesthood is made plain by the process of Ordination itself. As soon the first of its powers has been given it is used in the service of the Gospel and of the community of Christians.

The Offertory, the second part of the Act of Consecration of Man, follows. At its close the Ordination proceeds. First of all those who are becoming priests confirm the process of consecration by their own answer to a question. They are asked if they feel the significance of what they will have to do as priests. Then the second act of Ordination is performed. They are anointed with oil on the forehead, the hands and on the crown of the head and the words are spoken that bring with them the power to celebrate the Christian sacraments. Thereupon the chasuble is given to them as the sign of this power. This act is sealed by the invocation of the Trinity which is spoken three times, by the celebrant, by the one who receives the chasuble, and by the server for the congregation. Whereupon the celebrant, the server and the community of priests answer: 'Yea, so be it.' In this act, what happens in the process of Ordination is made clear. The substance and power is given by the divine world, from Father, Son and Holy Spirit through the acts and words of the celebrant. It is received and acknowledged by those who are consecrated, by the community of Christians and by the community of Christian priests.

At the close of the third part of the Act of Consecration of Man, the third act of the Ordination is performed. Those who are now consecrated are sent out to work in the name of Christ in the congregations. The celebrant lays their hands on the forehead and over the heart of each one. Thereupon they cover the chalice holding the consecrated wine and the paten with the consecrated bread and walk, holding them in their hands, in a circle round all the priests who are present. This done, they mount the pulpit and address the congregation, announcing to them the new priests as shepherds of souls, working in the name of Christ and calling on them to recognize them as such. In this act the relation of the priest is made clear to the two communities, to the community of those who celebrate the sacraments and to the community of those who receive them, or, in other words, of those who proclaim the Gospel and of those who hear it.

Following the Communion, the fourth part of the Act of Consecration of Man, words are spoken which recall the newly finished act of Ordination and point to the way it should work in human life in times to follow. The congregation is called upon to accompany the deeds of the newly-ordained priests and to help them. Ordination is a spiritual act performed once and for all. Once done, it can never be undone. However, it has the character that we have touched upon in many of our descriptions: something has been inaugurated; it is not yet complete. What is originated in the sacrament has to flow out into a whole lifetime of Christian work. Those who are consecrated receive in order to give, they are endowed with power in order to work, they are given grace in order to care for human souls.

The festival of Ordination includes the first celebration of the Act of Consecration of Man by the newly ordained priests. We have described above how the biretta is handed over as the symbol of office as the prelude to this celebration. Once the new priests have received this, have celebrated and given Communion to the congregation, they have entered into their office and task. They have received holy orders and have taken up their charge.

What happens?

In the Ordination of Priests, human work is transformed by a sacramental act. There is a phrase that was used at one time more frequently than it is now: 'to have a vocation.' This phrase implies that people felt themselves called to a particular work in the world by the guidance of God. Nowadays this aspect of human work is overshadowed by another which is summed up in the much more common phrase: 'to get a job.' The word 'job' implies a means of earning money, a means of setting one's self up in the world. Work can mean more than this, as one can hear in the way in which people speak of their satisfaction in doing a 'worthwhile job.' Deep within every human soul, though it may be buried away unnoticed, is a longing to work at something worthwhile. Sometimes it rises to the surface in an impulsive way and the most unexpected people want to change their established jobs and to devote themselves to work that is outwardly unprofitable but satisfying to their ideals and sense of purpose. Such people feel all at once that the longing for security and comfort is much less important than the deeper longing to fulfil something in the world by one's work. These are still the exceptional ones; in the mass of people this longing lives too, for it is part of the best in human nature, but it lives side by side with its opposite, the longing for security. This is the dilemma about work in which we are all involved today, unless we are fortunate enough to have the kind of job in which both these longings can be satisfied together.

The Sacrament of Ordination illumines this whole problem of human work by what is done within it for the work of the priest. It allows us to watch consciously the process of taking up work inspired by the spirit. There are three parts in the process: the calling, the empowering, and the sending out. Those who seek Ordination feel the calling, that is 'the vocation' coming to them from within their own hearts, from the minds of other people, including those who are already priests, and from the events of their destiny. When the Act of Consecration begins they are offered to God, the Ground of the World. They have been called by an impulse of the spirit, and their answer is to themselves. In this sense, the sacrament begins with the calling. Out of the calling evolves the act of giving power.

We could refer to this bestowal of power as 'enabling.' The ones who offer themselves are enabled to become celebrants; they are endowed with the grace to fulfil the sacraments. From the act of 'enabling' evolves the sending out. They are sent into the world to do the work to which they have been called and enabled. Through this threefold process an impulse having its origin in the spirit is transformed into work done in the world — in every sense as 'a job,' or rather one should say as a 'worthwhile job.'

The process is apparent in the work of the priest in its clearest form. However, it exists in other kinds of work, though it may be so little apparent that one may only begin to observe it through experiencing what happens in the ritual of Ordination. Through this process it can come about that in many forms of work, vocation can be combined with 'having a job.' The secret of making this possible is to have the courage to be confident that the spirit can and does work powerfully in the world, right down into the affairs of work and daily life. Then those who find the courage can take their problem of what work to do back to its beginning in the divine world, and look for their 'calling.' Having found it they will surely experience the aid of the spiritual world which through their destinies enables them to do the work they have chosen, and which can also be experienced as 'sending' them to the place and the people with whom they are to work. The Sacrament of Ordination is celebrated for only one kind of work, but because it is given to those who are to work as priests, all other human work is lifted up into its light, all other workers may seek the blessing that is poured out over divinely inspired human work.

What happens in the Ordination of Priests is that the way in which they work in the world is changed. Those who become priests are changed as workers, but something else happens also. They are changed in their human nature. Here again, it is true to say that what is done for the few with a special purpose, sheds its light upon all other human beings. Something is brought out and made effective through the consecration which is there in every human soul, although we are generally unaware of it. Let us look once again at the figure whom we have described as the pattern of all priesthood, John the Baptist. 'There was a man sent from God, whose name was John,' the Evangelist says of him (John 1:6). He is the pattern of the human being, in that he is always aware that he has come forth from God. He keeps alive his tie to the divine world and through this, he is able to do the work of God. At the baptism of Jesus, he stands, representing humanity, and speaks the words performs the acts which, from the earthly side, do what is required that the Son of God can enter the body of a man. John bears the grace of spirit that enables him to bring that which human souls may offer to partake in the working of the Trinity. The devotion of John and the presence of the Spirit within him are the hidden treasures of every human soul, born of God. This divine and human nature of the human being is made plain when the priest stands at the altar in vestments, representing all humanity. The secret love of God in the human being is the power that is brought out and confirmed in the consecration. Through it the priest may speak the words and perform the acts that may work within the working of God.

The Purpose of
The Christian Community

A few sentences were written in the introduction about the origin of The Christian Community. Now in conclusion something should be said briefly about its purpose. Its founders gave it a kind of subtitle: A movement for religious renewal. This is a true description but a very general one. How is such an aim put into practice? Communities or congregations of people are formed with the aim of helping Christ's healing work in the world. The foregoing chapters will have made it plain that the members of these congregations are people who wish to attend The Christian Community as their Church, and that there are ordained priests who work full-time within it. They receive Ordination for life in order that they can care for the work of The Christian Community. A threefold picture of the working of The Christian Community emerges from the Ordination: the celebration of the sacraments, the proclamation of Christianity and the care of souls. All these three tasks may also be thought of united in one: to create communities that carry the ever present working of Christ out into the lives of men and women and of the world.

Wherever The Christian Community exists, these tasks are the reason for its existence. As it is to be found in a number of different countries, the style of its life naturally changes from country to country, from place to place. Each one would require a separate description. Many new discoveries in congregational life have still to be made. The

Christian Community is young and flexible enough to change its ways easily, while the lasting purposes hold firm. The celebrations of the sacraments are festivals in themselves. The proclamation of Christianity is done by the spoken word in sermons, lectures and groups meeting for the study of the Bible or other relevant subjects. These are held from time to time, or conferences are arranged with concentrated courses. It is done by the written word in books and journals. There is religious instruction for children and young people which takes different forms according to the situation and possibilities of the respective congregations. The Christian festivals of the year form the basis of the programme of events in the congregations. Artistic activities are seen as an important part of the culture of The Christian Community and are cultivated where appropriate. All members and friends are, as individuals, the concern of the priests, and they are all free to ask for their help if and when they wish. Freedom is a practical experiment in The Christian Community. Members and friends are free to take what is offered and no claims and obligations are put upon them, although it is hoped that they will feel responsible for the continuing existence of The Christian Community and will help in such ways as they can to ensure it.

The Christian Community is supported financially solely by the gifts of its members and friends. The administrative and financial structures both within the congregations and within the regions in which the Community is organized are built up in ways that reflect the basic beliefs about the spiritual integrity of the individual.

Do others do not such things already? Are there not other Churches that might use the same words to describe their purpose as have been used here for The Christian Community? Such questions easily arise. A single glance at our world provides an answer. Can it be contended that there is too much religion, too much Christianity, that the older Churches have done all that is necessary? It would be much more true to say that Christianity must be much more powerfully practised, much better understood, if the chaos of today's world is to be changed into world order. What else will save the existence and the future of humanity?

The worth of The Christian Community, what it contributes to the world dilemma of our time, is something that those who meet it can only decide for themselves. Outwardly it is still a small community, though widely spread through the world. Many of its meeting-rooms and churches are modest. Nevertheless, we could think of Christianity's modest beginnings amongst the poor and disregarded in the Holy Land and then as a persecuted minority in the Roman world. The ultimate test can only be the question: where do we find the living presence of Christ now in our time? As we said at the beginning, the answer is: Come and see for yourself.

Epilogue

'What is man that thou art mindful of him?' (Ps.8:4) is the lasting, recurring question of the human soul which the Psalmist put with such unsurpassed clarity. It is an urgent matter today to find ways of asking this fundamental question again, and to find a way of hearing answers as fundamental as the question. We saw in the Prologue that such a change of perspective is needed if we are to see the sacraments as a part of our world. Speaking of them brings us in thought to the great questions of meaning and purpose, of origin and destination of the world and humanity.

These great questions about the human being brings forth another one as great. Let us return to one fact that was described early on in the Prologue, namely, that the human being is an unfinished creature, with its fulfilment in the future. Should the evolution of Man stop now, should it cease, leaving men and women to end as they are today, then the human being would be a cosmic failure, a reject in the world order. Hope for human beings lies in the future, in what still may become of them. But it would be untrue to assume that the future is a foregone conclusion, that the world progresses as reliably as an express train reaches its destination. There is plenty to show to the contrary in our own time. An author who wished to write a book today on the decline and fall of man would be able to collect a mass of material to support the theme. No, the future of humanity is an open question. And it is one that we ourselves have to answer. It is not a matter of finding out an answer, but of creating it. To the open question of their future, human beings themselves must create the answer.

Because of this question Christ came down to earth, became man and performed his deed on Golgotha. Because of this question he works on in the world today, showing to human beings the pattern of his purpose, offering them the strength to work towards it. We who are part of the great being of Man, who each bear the image of the truly human within us, are each of us engaged in helping to fashion the great answer that is to come. The sacraments are the opportunity to come to work together with Christ in community. Participating in the words and deeds of the sacraments in community, our individual souls, our single lives can become part of the great cosmic struggle for the Christian answer to the question of our existence.

What is this Christian answer? It is described in the Bible in the form of a picture, or rather a vision. The Old Testament begins with a great vision of the origin of Man; the New Testament closes with another great vision, the fulfilment of Man. The first vision is the Garden of Paradise, planted by God to be the dwelling-place of the first man and woman. The last vision is the New Jerusalem, the Holy City descending from the heavens to be the dwelling-place of the redeemed human souls. In the difference between the garden and the city is symbolized what happens between the origin and fulfilment of the human being. The garden was created by God. Adam and Eve lived there as his children until the serpent tempted them to the rebellious act which is described as the eating of the forbidden fruit. Then the garden was lost, the earth became wild and the human beings grew, as the stories in the Old Testament show, further and further away from God.

The city is shown in a vision to John, the Seer of the Apocalypse, who wrote down what he saw in the Book of

Revelation. He saw a city. The city is a potent symbol in the Bible. It symbolizes what human beings achieve together: the power to create that dwells within human community. This power can be put in the service of egotism and arrogance, as shown in the story of the Tower of Babel. The city of Babylon figures in the Book of Revelation as a symbol of evil. Now this symbol of the city receives a new, positive meaning. The city John saw was descending from heaven. As he looked his vision began to transform itself into something else: he saw the city becoming a living being, turning into the heavenly Bride, descending to meet the Bridegroom. Such a city cannot only be the work of human hands. What human beings have created in community will become part of God's creative work. It will not be built of dead stone that will one day turn to dust, as earthly cities are. It will be the dwelling of human beings, when they have risen again to be the sons and daughters of God.

Between the vision of the garden that was lost and that of the city that is to be built, there is the deed of Christ. Without it there would already be no future for the human being. The forces of egotism and arrogance would have triumphed. No communal work of building could be done. Because of it the future of humanity is still an open question, its fulfilment is still to come. Because of it, Christ is still present in our human world on earth, quickening his creating power in human souls. He is the divine Creator, who is creating our future from within us.

The sacraments are his words and deeds, spoken by a human voice, performed by human hands, witnessed and carried by human communities. They are the revelation of his presence. They fulfil from day to day what he himself promised in the words of the Gospel: 'and lo, I am with you always, to the close of the age' (Matt.28:20).